Rare Spiritual Robotics

Faith is the DNA code of God and Robotics is an analogy of this Rare Spiritual substance in motion on the earth.

John McCann

Copyright © 2013 by John McCann

Rare Spiritual Robotics
Faith is the DNA code of God and Robotics is an analogy of this Rare Spiritual substance in motion on the earth.
by John McCann

Printed in the United States of America

ISBN 9781628395808

All rights reserved solely by the author. The author guarantees all contents are original and do not infringe upon the legal rights of any other person or work. No part of this book may be reproduced in any form without the permission of the author. The views expressed in this book are not necessarily those of the publisher.

Unless otherwise indicated, Bible quotations are taken from The King James Version; The New Greek-English Interlinear New Testament, Translators: Robert K. Brown and Philip W. Comfort, Editor: J.D. Douglas. Copyright © 1990 by Tyndale House Publishers, Inc.; and The Greek New Testament: SBL Edition. Copyright © 2011 by Michael W. Holmes, Society of Biblical Literature.

www.xulonpress.com

Contents

Introduction vii
Dedication xv
Acknowledgments xvii

1. Junk Food for the Soul 19
2. The Disputed Border 36
3. The Analogy of a Robot 53
4. Old Testament Robots 81
5. New Testament Robots 96
6. Robots in Reverse 104
7. The Wiring and Currency of Denominations 140
8. Gospel Robots 155
9. A Desire for Robots 166
10. Natural Robots 184
11. Auxiliary Parts 194
12. Blessings 219

About the Author 229
Endnotes 231
Index of Scripture 239
Index 255

Introduction

In 2011 I completed a theological study program and was planning on continuing at another school. Meanwhile, I started writing. First came the fictional anecdote "*The Brazilian Church*" in Chapter eight. Next, I wrote my personal testimony in Chapter nine for family and friends. Then, I jotted down my theological views to a pastor of a church I was visiting.[1] If the pastor said, "*John, you would not be happy here, we believe differently,*" I was ahead of the curve. A statement that bothered me was, "*God does not make robots.*" This statement placed limitations on the creative ability and the sovereign control of the Lord (see Ps. 115:3). My disagreement was to be short, but I discovered a mark that I could aim at. The mark is:

- Christian perfection (see Matt. 5:48)
- The liberation of discipleship (see John 8:31-32)
- And the final goal of faith (see I John 3:2; Heb. 12:2).

Soon principles from Scripture revealed the robot analogy. I shared this with others and was advised to back off of the robot analogy. I agreed and prayed about the analogy. I labor to stay in the foundational print of Scripture and did not want to misrepresent the Lord Jesus Christ. Still, the thoughts kept coming, so I kept writing. When I mention robot, it is an analogy just as Jesus mentioned sheep as an analogy of His followers (see John 10). Like one pastor[2] illustrated, the power of Holy Spirit as a four-barrel carburetor: "robot" is

<u>not</u> to be taken literally. You might say, "*God does <u>not</u> make vessels, man makes vessels.*" However, the prophets Isaiah and Jeremiah as well as the apostle Paul used vessels as an analogy of humans in the hands of a sovereign God (see Isa. 64:8; Jer. 18:6; Rom. 9:21). Likewise, the robot analogy is about the control of Jesus toward His followers. The relationship between the Father and Son is mentioned, but it would be heresy to infer that Jesus is a Robot of His Father since a robot is a creation and Jesus always existed. However, man[3] is a creation (see Gen 1:27).

> (Usually the definite article "the" is placed in front of Holy Spirit. In this book, "the" in front of Holy Spirit is missing because the Person is meant when the article is absent. You would <u>not</u> write, "the John Doe," but "John Doe." As a general rule the article is present where the subject of the teaching is the Personality of the Holy Spirit.[4])

Concerning the contrast between robots and free will; here is what I am saying and <u>not</u> saying.)

- I am <u>not</u> saying that you cannot go here and there or do this or that. This is where most people live. This is living by sight or reason in the natural world (see Prov. 3:5b). These events are recorded in Scripture (see Gen. 3-Rev. 19).

- I am saying that the Lord can sovereignly control man. God does what He wills, even raising dead rotten flesh back to life (see John 11:43). This is rare, perhaps less than 1% of the entire population and less than 1% of the time. However, this is all He needs to accomplish His will and fulfill His purpose. These Spiritual events are recorded in Scripture.

Introduction

- I am saying that you can reach a level of discipleship where you can hear and obey Jesus uncontrolled by human will. This is <u>not</u> a pathway to salvation, since salvation is <u>not</u> of works. This is discipleship after salvation.

- I am <u>not</u> saying that Christians act like robots all the time. From the observation of history and current events, we often see the opposite.

- I am saying that the final state for all saints in heaven will be an obedient son or daughter, made in the image of God, similar to a robot, <u>not</u> exactly like a robot, but closer to a robot than a free agent.

- I am <u>not</u> saying that God makes robots. Man has a complex soul that can reason and act in the natural world.

- I am saying the analogy of a robot is appropriate when God controls man.

God made man. Man makes robots. Would man make a robot he could <u>not</u> control? Would God make a man He could <u>never</u> control? Let the apostle answer.

For we cannot but speak the things which we have seen and heard. Acts 4:20

Consider hypnosis, where man can neutralize the soul of another and control his speech and motion to a limited degree. Surely, God can do the same and more. God can easily control man like a robot; however, He chose to create a complex soul whereby man can reason and act. Spiritual robotics is rare, but necessary in order to preserve a remnant. Left alone, man sinks downward (see Rom. 1:21-32).

Concerning the contrast between the sovereignty of God and free will, it is <u>not</u> either one or the other that prevails. God sovereignly allows man's will in the natural world and sometimes He controls man (see Gen. 20:6). God does <u>not</u> have to force the will of man just as the owner of a safe does <u>not</u> have to force the door open. The Owner knows the combination to open the door (see Acts 16:14).

Man's goings *are* of the Lord, how can a man then understand his own way? Prov. 20:24

Within the book, the word "control" is used for "**authority**", "**power**", "**ability**" and "**all things are possible with God**." God does <u>not</u> have to force anything in His creation, but an unauthorized agent would use force to control (see John 10:1-3). "Control" is used to imply that God has the right to "make happen", as He wills, without force (see II Pet. 2:9). Man can pray, but God has the authority to allow or deny (see I Sam. 12:15-23). These mysteries of divine dynamics are dim to man, and frankly, none of man's business (see Luke 13:1-5; Acts 1:7; Rom. 9:20; I Cor. 13:12). A companion word "program" is used where God installs intelligence, revelation and ability into His creation in order to obtain His desired results (see Gen. 11:7-8; Job 38-41; Rom. 9:21).

There are a number of reasons for writing the book.

- Glorification: All things are possible with God (see Mark 10:27). God can control every aspect of His creation whenever He chooses. He does <u>not</u> have to force anything or anybody since He has the understanding and the authority over His creation to "make it happen". The glory of God is revealed through imputed faith, which allows God to program man (see Rom. 4:20). This is rare and man often rejects this principle of control, even when Scripture and history witness it.

- Caution: Implying that "*God does <u>not</u> make robots*" is presumptuous, since only the Creator knows what Christians will finally be like. We know that we will be like Jesus, Who spoke and acted in harmony with the Father (see Phil. 3:21; I John 3:2).

- Encouragement: After salvation, Christians led by Holy Spirit have the capacity of complete obedience and respond similar to a robot.

- Correction: Free will is limited. God created the will of man and the language of the Bible testifies to man being led, deceived and dominated by spiritual forces (see Eph. 6:12).

- Revelation: To reveal that thoughts, words and deeds outside the will of God have no Spiritual value.

- Witness: I will share my experiences in the culture and the church.

- Inspiration: I was inspired to write.

I considered using a pen name, like Dr. Robb Bott, which agrees with the "no recognition, all glory to God" concept, but declined because it agrees with the "deception from human reasoning" concept. The name of the book has evolved.

- The Robots of Jesus
- The Robot of Jesus Analogy
- Christian Perfection Using the Analogy of a Robot
- **Rare Spiritual Robotics**

The name "God Makes Perfect Children" was considered, but a similar title existed about the Christian Science movement.[5] Christian Science believe it's never God's will for anyone to suffer, be sick or die.[6] I believe that God refines and strengthens faith through suffering, sickness and death (see I Pet. 1:6-7).

Rare Spiritual robotics was chosen as the title. Rare means few people or a rare occurrence in time. Spiritual means controlled by God. Robotics means absolute sovereign acts. In six days, God created the heavens and the earth. Six days is rare compared to the total sum of history. The creation was by His Spirit, so it was Spiritual. The creation was robotics. Everything was done according to the design of the Creator. Next, rare Spiritual robotics continued with the rapture of Enoch and the dividing of the Red Sea (see Gen. 5:24, 14:21). Consider the rapture of the church in the twinkling of an eye (see I Cor. 15:52). These are all rare Spiritual robotics. They are not everyday, but rare, Spiritual and robotic, such as a born from above regenerated heart (see John 3:3; Titus 3:5). Due to the everyday "natural" activity, man can deny rare Spiritual robotics, and insist that God will not act against the will of man. God laughs at this absurdity (see Ps. 2).

Concerning the content of the book, I discuss free will in chapters one and two. If free will is your thing, consider the robot analogy in chapter three and step back to a position of obedience where you feel comfortable. Chapters four and five illustrate the robot analogy. Chapter six and eleven are theological in content with subject headings. In chapter seven and chapter nine, I expose some of my personal injustices to illustrate the carnal world and at times, the carnal church.

My favorite subjects within the book are:

- Faith (Chapter Three)
- Abraham (Chapter Four)
- The Soul Winner (Chapter Six)
- The Brazilian Church (Chapter Eight)
- The Rainbow Sky theory/picture (Chapter Ten)
- Willful Sin (Chapter Eleven)

The book is not solely about robotics. Scripture interpretation and personal observations are discussed, which was my original intent. The Word is Spiritual and a mind set on the Spiritual is life and peace (see John 6:63; Rom. 8:6).

Therefore, a proper interpretation is necessary. This is <u>not</u> Gnosticism, which hints that knowledge is a pathway to salvation (cf. I Cor. 8:1). Instead, proper interpretation benefits the fixed Spiritual nature (see Rom. 12:2). Incorrect doctrine will hinder the transition to a Spiritual-minded disciple. Therefore, man labors with proper interpretation while God does His will with Spiritual robotics. Nevertheless, the Spiritual realm that God controls is <u>not</u> contingent upon any proper interpretation. Within the book, you will encounter several places where I interpret from Scripture:

- Once saved, always saved, which I agree with,
- Today's methods of evangelism, which I disagree with and
- The annihilation of the unsaved, which I agree with.

The goal of the book is <u>not</u> for you to choose to become a robot of Jesus. A robot of Jesus is an analogy to illustrate how God can control and program His creation through faith. However, in chapter three, discipleship is discussed where you die to self and Holy Spirit leads you, similar to a robot of Jesus. I call this **beautification**. Indeed, the free will of man and the sovereignty of God have a long history of theological debate. My goal is to confirm the limited free will of man in the natural world and the Sovereign will of God in the nature and Spiritual worlds using the analogy of a robot. My hope is that the reader will be encouraged to study the Scriptures to see if these things are so.

Dedication

To God the Father of the Lord Jesus Christ, Who chose Victor Theodore McCann and Mary Edna McCann to bring forth physical life. And to Holy Spirit, Who brought forth Spiritual life.

Victor Theodore
McCann and John
Savannah Beach, Georgia

Mary Edna McCann
Augusta, Georgia

Acknowledgments

I would like to thank Mrs. Jean Barnes, Mrs. Peggy Frost, Mr. Brian Baldowski, Mr. Daniel Guidry and the folks at Xulon for editing and Mr. Michael Washer for two Photoshop drawings. Back cover photo by Portrait Innovations at Augusta Mall on August 21, 2013. These labors were in the natural realm of grammar and artistry, so recognition is appropriate (see Rom. 16:6; I Tim. 5:18).

Chapter One

Junk Food for The Soul

Earth has millions of square miles of land and water. The surface of earth is where man was designed to live. Unless man breaths oxygen from an alternate source, this is his space and he has been given a life sentence.

> **for dust thou** *art*, **and unto dust shalt thou return.** Gen. 3:19b

As fish were designed to live in water, man was designed to live by the laws of God. The law is Spiritual, just as God is Spirit. For some purpose, God created man with the ability to reason, which led to disobedience, which led to separation from the Spiritual, which led to death (see Gen. 2:16-17, 3:6). Now man is limited to the natural realm (see Ps. 8:6). Man is disconnected to the Spiritual realm unless God intervenes (see John 1:13). Natural man dies because he cannot continually obey the Spiritual laws that he was designed to live by. Man was designed to speak the truth, to be faithful to one wife, to not covet what others have and to serve God. Instead he obeys the law of sin and dies (see Rom 7:22-24). He is like a fish out of water (see John 4:14). He transgresses. He runs off the rails he was designed to run on. He misses the mark or sins. Therefore, he only exists for a brief period because he is deceived. Life on earth is like driving in a police bait car, a vehicle used by the police to capture car thieves. The vehicle has a "kill switch," which allows the police to remotely disable the engine and lock all doors from the inside, preventing escape. Life on earth is similar: you start driving, <u>not</u> knowing when the police will shut it down and lock the doors. Then you must appear before a Judge. Many go headfirst into life, like driving in a police bait car, believing that God has given them free will. However, every word and deed is recorded in books (see Rev. 20:12). Then life ends with judgment or pardon (see Heb. 9:27).

Free will is junk food for the soul. Free will is a euphoria that car thieves feel in a police bait car. Indeed, car thieves have free will to turn the steering wheel and the stereo dial for a brief period, but car thieves are a detriment to society. Likewise, free will has high natural appeal, but contains no Spiritual value and is a detriment to wholeness. Free will flies under the radar of any usefulness for the Kingdom of God. Free will is a misleading fallacy (see Jer. 23:16-17). Free will disconnects the flow of instructions from God in order to do one's own will, the essence of sin. In Christianity, free will advocates follow a road that leads to a dead-end, with a broken-hearted Jesus[1], tears rolling down His cheeks as He helplessly watches (cf. John 6:67-70, 17:2; II Cor. 13:3). Free will is defined as the power of directing our own actions without restraint by necessity or fate.[2] Has God given man free will without restraints? No, the restraints are:

- Holy Spirit
- Angels
- Physical laws of nature
- Law of sin
- Government
- Circumstances
- Our conscience
- Satan

Due to Holy Spirit, a Christian will experience different restraints than an unbeliever (see Acts 16:6). Due to angels, the direction of life can change (see Gen. 22:11-12; Ps. 91:11; Matt 2:13). An angel can give a message that the conscience cannot ignore. Due to the physical laws of nature, man cannot walk on water; walk through walls or float upward without assistance. The law of sin and death restrains man from freely choosing not to sin. Man is in bondage to sin just as the law of gravity pulls man down. Because of the established governments, a citizen of San Francisco, California, will experience different restraints than a citizen of Mecca, Saudi Arabia. Circumstances can dictate and override the human will. Circumstance can be an unavoidable path. After 14 years of service, quarterback Peyton Manning was released on March 7, 2012 from the Indianapolis Colts football team. Both Peyton and the owner, Jim Irsay, wanted Peyton to stay.[3] However, the following circumstances did not allow Peyton to stay:

- A NFL salary cap (120.6 million)
- A recovering neck injury (Peyton)
- The Colt's first round draft pick (2-14 record)
- A young quarterback (Andrew Luck) entering the NFL

Circumstances are walls or boundaries on the landscape of life. When circumstances dictate, the victim may lie to justify his or her prior statements. Others have their resources depleted and do not have a choice to continue. The right to choose becomes extinct. Free will is gone.

The most common restraint is the conscience— "judgment of right and wrong; or the faculty, power or principle within us, which decides on the lawfulness or unlawfulness of our own actions and affections, and instantly approves or condemns them."[4] The consciousness of good and evil was implanted in the first parents when they disobeyed God (see Gen. 2:7). Perhaps, the first child, Cain, demonstrated a severed conscience and he was unable to deter wrong (see I Tim. 4:2; I John 3:12). This is similar to a rare psychopathic personality— "an emotionally and behaviorally disordered state characterized by perception of reality except for the individual's social and moral obligations. This state is often characterized by the pursuit of immediate personal gratification in criminal acts, drug addiction or sexual perversion."⁵ Religions, including certain doctrines and traditions within Christianity were established to satisfy the conscience. Within Christianity, the conscience can be purged from dead works, implying that traumatic acts that hinder peace can be forgotten by the individual, similar to shock therapy in the medical world (see Heb. 9:14). Still, God has given man a conscience, <u>not</u> unrestrained free will. The conscience allows God to judge man. Man knows what is right and does <u>not</u> have an excuse. However, the conscience is within the corrupt soul, which craves praise when it does good and silence when it does evil (see Matt. 6:1-2; John 3:19-20).

Satan is a deceptive restrainer. "Scripture represents man as one who is <u>not</u> only bound, wretched, captive, sick and dead, but in addition to his other miseries is afflicted with this misery of blindness through the agency of Satan. Therefore man believes himself to be free, happy, unfettered, able, well and alive."⁶ Satan is the enemy and adversary of Christians (see Acts 13:10; I Pet. 1:8). Satan even restrained the apostle Paul from traveling to Thessalonica (see I Thes. 2:18). Concerning evil, Satan prefers to broadcast it like a roaring lion instead of being silent (see I Pet. 5:8).

Whenever someone does <u>not</u> accept these restraints, all sorts of ungodly behavior can manifest itself such as anger and rage, resulting in this untoward generation (see Acts 2:30). Contrast love, which does <u>not</u> insist on its own, but bears, believes, hopes and endures (see I Cor. 13:5,7).

> *God, grant me the serenity to accept the things I cannot change, The courage to change the things I can, And wisdom to know the difference.*⁷

What about the will itself? Man does have a will (see John 1:13). The will of man has limited ability in the temporal or material realm and no ability in the Spiritual. However, the will of man (from the corrupt soul inherited through Adam) does not function properly. The will of man is in bondage to sin, not free. Freedom comes when Jesus makes man free from sin.

> **If the Son therefore shall make you free, ye shall be free indeed.** John 8:36

Meanwhile, God observes and records all of man's activity from heaven. All shall be held accountable.

> **Neither is there any creature that is not manifest in his sight: but all things *are* naked and opened unto the eyes of him with whom we have to do.** Heb. 4:13

Wisdom is a realization that all words and deeds will be accounted for and brought before God. Man shall give an account. Every work shall be judged (see II Cor. 5:10; Rev. 20:12). Meanwhile, free will is a disguise to hide behind. Free will hints at no accountability. Man becomes comfortable in this present world and assumes comfort and freedom will always be. However, Scripture uncovers the disguise. Man behaves according to his nature. Things a Christian considers truth, an unbeliever considers a lie and vice versus.

The unbeliever

> **Ye are of *your* father the devil, and the lusts of your father ye will do.** John 8:44a

> **Wherein in time past ye walked according to the course of this world, according to the prince of the power of the air, the spirit that now worketh in the children of disobedience:** Eph. 2:2

The Christian

My sheep hear my voice, and I know them, and they follow me: John 10:27

For as many as are led by the Spirit of God, they are the sons of God. Rom. 8:14

Works of free will do <u>not</u> agree with the Christian's Spiritual nature. Even Jesus confessed that He did <u>not</u> come to do His own human will but the will of the Father (see John 6:38).

For that ye *ought* to say, If the Lord will, we shall live, and do this, or that. James 4:15

Why has God given man a human will? The human will allows man to consider his shortcomings in order for God to reveal His grace by redeeming man and manifesting His power (see Rom. 7). The human will is made in the image of God, but falls short of the glory of God (see Gen. 1:26; Rom. 3:23). Meanwhile, free will is like a robot moving his arms and legs, and going about to and fro, but <u>not</u> accomplishing any meaningful tasks. This is illustrated in Scripture, where Martha moved around and was troubled while Mary sat at Jesus' feet hearing the Word (see Luke 10:38-42). Martha was exercising her will while Mary was hearing God's Word and desiring His will. Free will is like walking on a road with potholes while the will of God leads to walking on a street of gold (see Rev. 21:21). Free will is like a football coach calling an offensive play from the sidelines while all eleven players do what they think is best to advance the ball. Christian free will advocates proclaims, "*Yes I have a Bible, but God has given me free will.*" Free will implies detachment from any restraints beyond the borders of self. You would <u>not</u> want to live in a world where man was allowed free will without restraints. A free will experiment[8] was granted in the days of Noah. God relaxed His intervention and man degenerated to the point where "**every imagination of the thoughts of his heart** *was* **only evil continually.**" Man had forsaken the principles he was designed to live by. God saw the results and was sorry He had made man (see Gen. 6:5-6).

Uday Hussein, (son of Saddam Hussein, a former president of Iraq), was granted free will in virtually all of Iraq. One day Uday happened to cross paths with a newlywed couple at a hotel in Iraq. Uday had the husband restrained while he raped the wife. The wife was so disgusted that she jumped off the balcony and fell several stories to her death. She did not want to live in a world where such free will was allowed.[9] Jesus understood the depths of unrestrained free will. While walking to His crucifixion, He told the women not to weep for Him, but for themselves and their children.

The days are coming when barren and childless women will be considered blessed. Others will cry for the mountains to fall on them and the hills to cover them (see Luke 23:28-31). Unrestrained free will breeds evil. Whether free will has become the new religion, a stronghold that exalts itself above the knowledge of God, idolatry, blindness or heresy, I do not know. In certain circles, it has gone unchallenged. People like it and accept it.

Free Will and Salvation

Man possesses limited free will in the natural world, but nil free will in the Spiritual world (see Ps. 8:6-8). The Spiritual world belongs to God. Spiritual laws are different from natural laws (see Rom. 8:2). Man sees that he can operate in the natural world and assumes he has the same privilege in the Spiritual. In the natural, you select your clothes and what you are having for dinner. Why not choose where you are going to spend eternity? The problem is that **the carnal mind** *is* **enmity against God: for it is not subject to the law of God, neither indeed can be**. (Rom. 8:7).

Rare Spiritual Robotics

Some strongly believe in free will concerning Spiritual salvation. One minister said, "*The only one who can convert you is yourself. God cannot save you without your permission. That's how much freedom He has given you.*"[10] Another minister wrote, "*Here's the thing. Jesus can do a lot of things but he cannot, he will not, force us to choose Him, to choose life or to choose new beginnings. Only we can do that.*"[11]

This is salvation— American style:

- I went to a meeting...
- I walked forward...
- I knelt down at an old fashioned altar...
- I was lead to the Lord by the preacher...
- I repented...
- I confessed my sin...
- I accepted...
- I gave my heart...

This is salvation— heavenly style:

- He came to me. (Luke 19:10; John 3:17,19)
- He drew me. (John 6:44)
- He said live. (Ezek. 16:6)
- He made me alive in Christ. (Eph. 2:5)
- He raised me up. (Eph. 2:6)

- He saved me by grace, <u>not</u> work, lest I boast. (Eph. 2:8-9)
- He imparted faith as a gift. (Eph. 2:8)
- He chose and accepted me. (Eph. 1:4; Rom. 8:1)
- He gave me a new heart. (II Cor. 5:17)

Can man be saved through free will? The disciples asked Jesus who could be saved. Jesus replied, "**With men** *it is* **impossible, but not with God**" (see Mark 10:27). The question may be, "*Is the will of man off limits to God?*" I answer, "*No.*" Others answer, "*Yes, God will respect your will.*"

> **Jesus answered and said unto him, Verily, verily, I say unto thee, Except a man be born again, he cannot see the kingdom of God.** John 3:3

Why did Jesus describe entrance into the Kingdom this way? You do <u>not</u> choose your biological parents, neither do you choose your Spiritual parents. A human embryo virtually has no will. The involuntary brain and muscle activity start functioning. With these activities, the human will is bypassed. The Spiritual birth is similar. It bypasses the human will and creates a new creation in Christ Jesus. The human will does <u>not</u> want to be saved, so God changes the nature and then man's will is to call on the Name of the Lord, just as a baby cries after physical birth (see Rom. 3:11, 10:13).

> **As thou knowest not what is the way of the Spirit, nor how the bones do grow in the womb of her that is with child: even so thou knowest not the works of God who maketh all.** Eccl. 11:5

People like free will. After Sunday school, I showed the teacher the Scripture, "**Which were born, not of blood, nor of the will of the flesh, nor of the will of man, but of God**" (John 1:13). The teacher replied with a brazen look, "*I* *still believe in free will.*" Once the concrete has hardened on someone's belief, it often becomes permanent. "They simply cling tenaciously to their belief no matter what the evidence may be against it."[12] Seeing truth on paper is a physical activity. Hearing truth is a physical activity. Believing truth (faith) is a divine activity.

> **The wind bloweth where it listeth, and thou hearest the sound thereof, but canst not tell whence it cometh, and whither it goeth: so is every one that is born of the Spirit.** John 3:8

When a strong wind comes, can you choose to keep your hat on? Can you keep your hair in place by exercising free will? You can hear the sound and see the results, but you cannot control it. You cannot tell where it came from or where it is going. People do <u>not</u> like that. They want control to exercise their free will concerning salvation, yet Jesus can control the wind (see Mark 4:39).

From the soul that we inherited through Adam, it is most difficult to accept the will of God toward our loved ones that are <u>not</u> saved or born again. We cry out:

- I want them to be saved. . .
- I want them to know Jesus. . .
- I don't want them to go to hell. . .
- I can't pray enough about them. . .

I am <u>not</u> saying that Jesus will <u>not</u> save your loved one or that you should <u>not</u> pray for them (see Luke 18:1-8). I am saying that you must love Jesus more than you love those here on earth (see Matt. 10:37). You love Him by obedience and acceptance of His will. Maturity is when you accept His will above your strong corrupt will for your loved ones (see Gen. 22:1-18). Do you love Jesus more than your loved ones here on earth (see John 21:15)? Accepting Jesus is <u>not</u> an act of your will toward salvation, but an act of your will toward love and obedience to His will after salvation. This can be difficult due to our emotional nature.

Free Will and Daily Life

Free will is holding onto the natural and denying the Spiritual. For a Christian, the day should begin sitting at the breakfast table, hearing the daily plans from Spiritual Father. This involves reading Scripture, prayer and determining what God has placed in your heart versus doing your own free will.

Wisdom is following the passion(s) that God has placed in your heart (see Ps. 37:4). God will implant a desire within ladies' hearts to birth and nurture children. God will implant a desire to serve in the military. I desire to learn Hebrew and Greek words. Trusting in free will is foolish (see Prov. 28:26). Test the spirits to see if they are of God (see Acts 4:19; I John 4:1). For example, music is loved by virtually all. Pick up a musical instrument and learn to play a G and C (the peanut butter and jelly combination of music). If something within you reveals, *"You can do this,"* you should be able to play. What is within you is the path that is planned by God. What is within you is based upon your nature, whether the nature of God or the nature of the god of this world (see Eph. 2:2).

Suppose you need to travel from Augusta, Georgia to Columbia, South Carolina (see John 4:4; Rom. 1:10). The government has provided Interstate 20 that leads right into Columbia. Likewise, God has provided a path for His elect and Satan has provided a path for his group. Your nature determines whose child you are and what path you take. You either struggle or accept Satan's influences (see Eph. 6:12). For example, a night on the town will vary based upon your nature and calling (see I Cor. 7:17). Therefore, do not let the falsehood of free will entertain you. It does have appeal. It is easy to understand. Free will sits in front of you every day, but it should be denied. Beware. The will of man can be blind (see Matt. 15:14).

> **Know ye not, that to whom ye yield yourselves servants to obey, his servants ye are to whom ye obey; whether of sin unto death, or of obedience unto righteousness?** Rom. 6:16

What is the value of free will? The book of Ecclesiastes records the experiences of King Solomon. Solomon was great in wisdom, wealth and power. For a limited season, Solomon exercised his free will in virtually everything natural (under the sun) without any restraints from man or God.

Solomon had free will to create his own meaning and purpose. Solomon leaned on his own understanding and let free will direct his path (cf. Prov. 3:5-7). Solomon built idols, indulged in wine and women, and then used his wisdom to consider life's circumstances and the meaning of it all (see II Kings 23:13). No value was found. No profit was made.

> **Vanity of vanities, saith the Preacher, vanity of vanities; all is vanity. What profit hath a man of all his labour which he taketh under the sun?** Eccl. 1:2-3

Solomon tested all the roads and avenues of free will in order to establish a principle that man is obligated to God. A privileged few may have a large stage to exercise free will "**under the sun**" for a season, but this has no value in the Kingdom of heaven above the sun. Under the sun is the natural realm. Above the sun, God controls the Spiritual realm. Solomon concluded that all of life's choices would be brought to the light of judgment. The whole purpose of man is to keep the commandments of God. That is the meaning of life. Only the work of the Lord is <u>not</u> in vain (see I Cor. 15:58).

> **Let us hear the conclusion of the whole matter: Fear God, and keep his commandments: for this *is* the whole *duty* of man. For God shall bring every work into judgment,**

> **with every secret thing, whether** *it be* **good, or whether** *it be* **evil.** Eccl. 12:13-14

Unlike Solomon, advocates of free will may <u>not</u> have the wisdom to realize its vanity. They may <u>not</u> have a calling from God and do <u>not</u> experience the directing of Holy Spirit. The Church in Laodicea believed in free will. Then God informed them how blind they had become.

> **You say, 'I am rich; I have acquired wealth and do not need a thing.' But you do not realize that you are wretched, pitiful, poor, blind and naked.** Rev. 3:17

Some reason that life without choices is meaningless. This may be in the natural realm. For example, a husband has learned that his wife must make all the choices, and if <u>not</u>, the wife makes life miserable. The husband's role is to add to the financial resources that his wife controls. He feels meaningless which is still better than miserable.

However, that is <u>not</u> the case with God. All of God's plans are for our benefit to make life better. Doing the will of the Lord is meaningful and joyful, even the death on the cross (see Matt. 25:21; Heb. 12:2). However, if a wife can neutralize the will of her husband, so that he obeys her decisions to a tee, can the Lord <u>not</u> do the same and more?

Free Will and the Unsaved

Will God ask you to do something you are <u>not</u> able to do? Yes. He wants to show your limitations. Will God expect you to do something you are <u>not</u> able to do? No. Will God empower you to do something you are <u>not</u> able to do? Yes. Consider the nation of Israel. Through the law came the knowledge of sin to natural-unsaved man. However, <u>not</u> all of Israel was God's children. Many were unsaved and walked in the flesh (see Rom. 9:6-8).

And if it seem evil unto you to serve the LORD, choose you this day whom ye will serve; Joshua 24:15a

In the Old Testament Joshua gives the people a choice. This appears to imply free will, but actually reveals man's inability to serve God. Here we see an example of man's inability due to his fallen nature. Man could not choose life, because his fallen nature tilted toward disobedience and death. Joshua continues to speak.

And Joshua said unto the people, Ye cannot serve the LORD: for he *is* a holy God; Joshua 24:19a

God was setting the stage. Another Prophet was needed, the Messiah. The people of Israel were chosen to bring forth the law and the Messiah, but not all of Israel was saved (see John 8:44; Rom. 9:6).

In the New Testament, Romans 1:24-28 appears to imply free will toward the unsaved and states that God gave them up to uncleanness, vile affections and a reprobate mind. This appears to imply they have free will to do whatever they want. However, the will of God is seen first to allow them to act according to their nature. Yet even the willful disobedience of the unsaved is temporary and hopeless (see Eph. 2:12).

But after thy hardness and impenitent heart treasurest up unto thyself wrath against the day of wrath and revelation of the righteous judgment of God; Who will render to every man according to his deeds: To them who by patient continuance in well doing seek for glory and honour and immortality, eternal life: But unto them that are contentious, and do not obey the truth, but obey unrighteousness, indignation and wrath, Tribulation and

anguish, upon every soul of man that doeth evil, of the Jew first, and also of the Gentile; Rom. 2:5-9

Every soul, with his or her will, belongs to the Lord and He will judge in righteousness (see Ezek. 18:4; Jer. 11:20). The sins of those not written in the Lamb's book of life will suffer in the lake of fire until the wrath and justice of God is satisfied (see Luke 16:23-25). Then they will perish or be annihilated (see John 3:16).

Conclusion

The Creator can do what He wants with His creation.

for He maketh his sun to rise on the evil and on the good, and sendeth rain on the just and on the unjust. Matt. 5:45b

During this earthly life, the ungodly can suffer and the godly can suffer. The ungodly can live in peace and the godly can live in peace. The ungodly can die early and the godly can die early. The ungodly can live long and the godly can live long. The general principle is that the ungodly suffer and die early while the godly live in peace and die full of days. From Scripture and world history, there are times when man operates with little or no intervention from God, while other times God puts His hand down.

O Jerusalem, Jerusalem, *thou* that killest the prophets, and stonest them which are sent unto thee, how often would I have gathered thy children together, even as a hen gathereth her chickens under *her* wings, and ye would not! Matt. 23:37

In context, Jerusalem in the Scripture above was under the old covenant of obedience. The Scripture hints that man can limit God by his choices, but in the context of all Scripture, the case is lost (see Ezek. 36:24). However, He sometimes expresses a wish for that which He does not sovereignly bring to pass.[13] In the Scripture above, the free will of man is proven to be faulty. God gave Israel a place at the top of nations, an honorable religion and a beautiful temple in Jerusalem. Still, the will of man was unable to connect with the will of God.

The natural man in Adam could not serve God and instead choose to kill the prophets with the messages from God. Jesus is acknowledging that the old covenant does not work without faith (see Heb. 8:8). Jesus had to do some more work on their hearts (see Jer. 31:33). The idea that God has given man free will and honors his choices without intervening and without judgment is misleading. The record-keeping ability and integrity of God will be revealed when He judges every word and deed (see Matt. 12:36; Rom. 2:5-6). Everything is connected or disconnected until God puts all things in order. In the flesh, we do have the ability to sin or miss the mark. In the Spirit, we cannot sin. God is Spirit and walking in the Spirit is doing His will. In the natural realm we have limited will. In the Spiritual realm we have no will, because God controls the Spiritual. When God controls us, we can do all things according to His will.

Alongside Holy Spirit, total obedience to Jesus, is possible. A servant should do what is expected. This is Christian perfection, expecting no praise from others. Still, it takes discipline. One of the primary tasks is to renew the mind with the Word of God in order to understand the will of God. The task is to put commands in the memory bank in order to keep the burden light and the yoke easy so that meaningful acts are performed for the glory of God (see Matt. 11:30). The goal should be to limit sinning (choosing and making decisions against the will of God) and instead be obedient in thought, word and deed. The only One who has free will is God (see Rom. 9:11; Heb.

4:13). God cannot grant free will for man without an indictment for the destruction of all.

> **I tell you, Nay: but, except ye repent, ye shall all likewise perish.** Luke 13:3

Christians start with milk and grow by eating solid food (see Heb. 5:12-14). I am concerned about those who plunge headfirst into life believing in free will. Christian free will advocates pray for God to bless their will, instead of praying that His will be done. I was so indoctrinated in free will that it took several years to renew my mind and shake off the myth. Scripture provided a different perspective. In the garden, Eve plunged headfirst and ate of the tree of the knowledge of good and evil. Next, sin entered the world as Adam ate. In the garden, God allowed man to act. The result was death. I pray that God would be in control and His will be done in the earth (see Matt. 6:20; Rom. 8:14). The opposite is for man to be in control, which is the foundation of free will, the junk food for the soul. The effects of this junk food is seen today and throughout history.

Chapter Two

The Disputed Border

The disputed border is the invisible area where the heart of man and the Spirit of God meet. Neither God nor Christians dispute the location of the border. The location is the intangible area where the heart of man and the Spirit of God meet. The dispute involves the choice to cross the border and the direction of flow. God does not dispute the border crossing. Only Christians dispute the border crossing. Christians dispute salvation. Free will Christians believe that man initiates salvation. Sovereign will Christians believe that God initiates salvation. Christians dispute service and behavior. Free will Christians believe that everyone chooses his or her path. Sovereign will Christians believe that God decides (see Acts 9; Rom. 1:1).

I am a sovereign will Christian. I do not see in Scripture or from the observation of man's behavior, any Spiritual ability in man. Man's spiritual container is empty due to separation. God must pour Spiritual power into man's container or nothing Spiritual happens. The border crossing from God to man is not contingent upon anything or any merit within man. Otherwise, it would not be grace. Therefore, God has to cross the border to man. God crossed the border and created man from the earth (see Gen. 2:7). Man went his own way and fell (see Gen. 3:1-7). God crossed the border and judged man (see Gen. 3:14-19). Man continued to go his way and the earth became corrupt. God crossed the border and saved Noah and his family (see Gen. 6-8). Man re-populated the earth (see Gen. 8). Man sought unity and tried to cross the border to God by building a tower to heaven (see Gen. 11:1-9). God said "*no*" to man's plan because it is God that has to cross the border to man, not the other way around.

God crossed the border and established a religion and the nation of Israel. Man distorted the religion. God looked for a man to stand in the gap and could not find one. God crossed the border and sent His Son to redeem man with a better covenant. Man crucified His Son. God crossed the border and sent Holy Spirit to change the nature of man. Man established religion to control this event. Meanwhile, God continues to cross the border even though man does not understand (see John 3:8).

> **As thou knowest not what is the way of the spirit,** *nor* **how the bones** *do grow* **in the womb of her that is with child: even so thou knowest not the works of God who maketh all.** Eccl. 11:5

Concerning Salvation

Natural man is dead in sin and separated from God. The signal from God to the dead spirit of man is similar to an involuntary signal from the soul of a newborn baby that starts the lungs breathing. As the will of a newborn baby is bypassed that starts breathing, so the will of man is bypassed that regenerates the Spirit. Man is born again (see John 3:3). Whether a manmade robot has an internal battery or a remote control that transmits the power from a remote location, someone has to switch the power on. A robot is helpless in flipping the power switch on. Neither can a natural man bring life to his dead spiritual nature. Usually this happens during the preaching of the Word in order for the Spirit to find nourishment. Only God can make a Spiritual decision. Therefore, salvation is like the first robotic command from heaven to turn the power switch on and regenerate the nature of a natural man. This regeneration or born again action by God is called election. Christians dispute election.

1. Free will Christians believe that God crosses the border into everyone's heart at least one time in everyone's life and the individual chooses whether to invite or accept Jesus as his or her Savior.
2. Another group of free will Christians believe that the natural sinner must turn toward God and repent. When the sinner does this, God crosses the border and changes his or her nature.
3. **Sovereign will Christians believe that God crosses the border and chooses His elect and they cannot resist His irresistible grace.**

The first two disputes have partial Scriptural support and a lot of rational support. The first two honor men and create an image of God that is comfortable. I agree with the third because of comprehensive Scriptural support. The below Scripture is one example.

> **Unto you first God, having raised up his Son Jesus, sent him to bless you, in turning away every one of you from his iniquities.** Acts 3:26

Paige Patterson, a free will Christian, states that election is the most hated doctrine of the church.[1] John Calvin, a sovereign will Christian, states that election can be very sweet fruit.[2] Beliefs about election reveal where your religion is centered: man as a free agent or God as a sovereign Creator. Some believe that free will determines salvation, while others believe the will of God determines salvation. One person says, "*I absolutely believe in free will*," while another says, "*The Lord can do whatever He wills with His creation.*" However, both might agree that the Lord chooses certain sinners that we would stay clear of (see Acts 9:13). The Lord's choice of His elect is <u>not</u> based upon anything within the individual because He is <u>not</u> a respecter of persons (see Rom. 9:11; Acts 10:34). This is the opposite of the man's method and therefore man is unable to understand and can hate the election of God.

Man wants an even playing field where everyone has the same opportunity to choose God. God looks down from heaven and sees an even playing field. All have sinned. There is none righteous, <u>not</u> even one (see Rom. 3:10, 23). However, Scripture does hint that God chooses His elect from the poor and limits His choice of the wise (see Jam. 2:5; I Cor. 1:26-28). Still, there is no acceptable conduct from man that determines election. Election prevents any flesh from glorying (see I Cor. 1:29). Christians are predestined by the will of God through ways we cannot understand, <u>not</u> by the will of man (see John 1:13; Rom. 11:33). Original sin from Adam resulted in a dead spiritual nature that cannot do anything to draw or entice the Spirit of God to cross the border and regenerate the dead spirit. The will of man does <u>not</u> desire God, being blinded by the god of this world. Although unsaved natural man has a conscience of right and wrong, he cannot know God without the Spirit of God.

Therefore, God must initiate the change of nature. Once the nature has been changed, the Christian will call upon the Name of the Lord and acknowledge his or her new nature. This is based on Scripture, observation and personal experience. Some Scriptures appear problematic with this view, but are resolved with other Scriptures. Free will Christians dispute this, believing salvation occurs in reverse order. "**Whosoever will call on the Name of the Lord will be saved**" (Rom. 10:13). The will of God is that all be saved and once man is willing, God crosses the border and regenerates the nature. This is a comfortable view since God does <u>not</u> appear to choose one and reject the other, but this view places the burden on the sinner to "make it happen". Some Scriptures are privately interpreted to support this view (see Rom. 10:13; I Tim. 2:4; II

Pet. 3:9). And this view is supported by rational thinking and is popular today.

Man does have choice in the natural realm; however, salvation or Spiritual regeneration is a miracle by God, the same as a healing of lameness, blindness or deafness that man cannot choose to make happen. It would be nice if everyone had the ability to choose God, but Scripture reveals man cannot choose God due to his separated nature in Adam. Nevertheless, the message today is that you need to respond to what God has already done. You must reach out and make Jesus the Lord of your life. You need to give your heart to Jesus. (This sounds like an "organ donor" check mark on your driver's license.) No, Jesus must change your heart. The popular message proclaims that God is not going to force Himself on you. You must be willing. God is not going to act against your will. I like this message and people might get saved, but it is not how God saves people. How can you say that you made Jesus the Lord of your life and not boast? This does not give God all the glory and power. I have a problem harmonizing today's message with Scripture.

> **Which were born, not of blood, nor of the will of the flesh, nor of the will of man, but of God.** John 1:13

Here is an example of the disputed border concerning salvation. Pastor John Hagee of Cornerstone Church has a series titled, *Seven People God cannot save*. The title implies that God cannot cross the border for certain people. The apostle Paul described himself as the chief sinner (see I Tim. 1:15). Therefore, Paul was further from the mark of the seven people in pastor Hagee's list. Consider the Scripture below, which describes a salvation event.

> **But the righteousness which is of faith speaketh on this wise, Say not in thine heart, Who shall ascend into heaven? (that is, to**

> **bring Christ down** *from above*:**) Or, Who shall descend into the deep? (that is, to bring up Christ again from the dead.) But what saith it? The word is nigh thee, even in thy mouth, and in thy heart: that is, the word of faith, which we preach; That if thou shalt confess with thy mouth the Lord Jesus, and shalt believe in thine heart that God hath raised him from the dead, thou shalt be saved. For with the heart man believeth unto righteousness; and with the mouth confession is made unto salvation.** Rom. 10:6-10

A private interpretation of the Scripture above would lean toward man initiating salvation. However the full context reveals that God initiates the transition. Their belief depends upon a preacher being sent by God.

> **How then shall they call on him in whom they have not believed? and how shall they believe in him of whom they have not heard? and how shall they hear without a preacher? And how shall they preach, except they be sent? as it is written, How beautiful are the feet of them that preach the gospel of peace, and bring glad tidings of good things!** Rom. 10:14-15

The words of the prophet Isaiah (Esaias) reveal that God chooses those who did <u>not</u> seek Him. This is very bold and contrary to reasoning. This removes the control from man and people do <u>not</u> feel comfortable with losing control. This states that salvation is <u>not</u> contingent on man.

> **But Esaias is very bold, and saith, I was found of them that sought me not; I was**

> **made manifest unto them that asked not after me.** Rom. 10:20

Therefore, concerning who initiates salvation, Christians dispute the border crossing. Free will Christians claim that man has a free will and God does not make robots. Man does have a will, but God also has a will, which is revealed in Scripture.

> **Thou wilt say then unto me, Why doth he yet find fault? For who hath resisted his will? Nay but, O man, who art thou that repliest against God? Shall the thing formed say to him that formed** *it***, Why hast thou made me thus?** Rom. 9:19-20

A statement of God initiating salvation is difficult to place within your denomination's statement of beliefs, to see on a church's web site or for a seminary professor to teach, since students expect explanations and answers. The ways of God man can dispute, but not always discover.

> **O the depth of the riches both of the wisdom and knowledge of God! how unsearchable** *are* **his judgments, and his ways past finding out!** Rom. 11:33

Some appeal to God's love, implying that He has chosen everyone if they will believe (see John 3:16). Is it possible for God to love someone and not extend His arm of salvation? Yes.

> **And when he was gone forth into the way, there came one running, and kneeled to him, and asked him, Good Master, what shall I do that I may inherit eternal life? And Jesus said unto him, Why callest thou me good?** *there is* **none good but one,** *that is***, God. Thou**

knowest the commandments, Do not commit adultery, Do not kill, Do not steal, Do not bear false witness, Defraud not, Honour thy father and mother. And he answered and said unto him, Master, all these have I observed from my youth. Then Jesus beholding him <u>loved him</u>, and said unto him, One thing thou lackest: go thy way, sell whatsoever thou hast, and give to the poor, and thou shalt have treasure in heaven: and come, take up the cross, and follow me. And he was sad at that saying, and went away grieved: for he had great possessions. And Jesus looked round about, and saith unto his disciples, How hardly shall they that have riches enter into the kingdom of God! And the disciples were astonished at his words. But Jesus answereth again, and saith unto them, Children, how hard is it for them that trust in riches to enter into the kingdom of God! It is easier for a camel to go through the eye of a needle, than for a rich man to enter into the kingdom of God. And they were astonished out of measure, saying among themselves, Who then can be saved? And Jesus looking upon them saith, With men *it is* **impossible, but not with God: for with God all things are possible.** Mark 10:17-27

The rich man knew how sins were forgiven. He wanted to inherit eternal life, a completely different work of God. Jesus loved this rich man because love is His nature, yet He did <u>not</u> extend His arm of salvation (see Isa. 53:1). We know that giving up wealth does <u>not</u> merit salvation. He told His disciples that it is hard for those who have riches to enter the kingdom of God. They did <u>not</u> understand. He told them that it is hard for those who trust in riches to enter the kingdom of God. They did _not_ understand. He concluded that it is impossible for man to do anything for salvation. Therefore, the ability to cross the disputed border does _not_ come from man. We arrive at the question the disciples asked: "***who then can be saved?***" Today, the answer is generally anyone whom is willing to open his or her heart and receive Jesus as their Savior.

This is a comfortable position and understandable. It is _not_ popular to say with man it is impossible, unless you are bold (see Rom. 10:20). Other questions arise that are beyond our understanding. It is _not_ wise to reason that some people cannot be saved or that God is unjust in His choice of one over the other. God can do what He wants with His creation and be just. Is it possible for God to love a rich man and extend His arm of salvation? Yes.

> **And *Jesus* entered and passed through Jericho. And, behold, *there was* a man named Zacchaeus, which was the chief among the publicans, and he was <u>rich</u>. And he sought to see Jesus who he was; and could not for the press, because he was little of stature. And he ran before, and climbed up into a sycamore tree to see him: for he was to pass that *way*. And when Jesus came to the place, he looked up, and saw him, and said unto him, Zacchaeus, make haste, and come down; for to day I must abide at thy house. And he made haste, and came down, and received him joyfully. And when they saw *it*, they all murmured, saying, That he was gone to be guest with a man that is a sinner. And Zacchaeus stood, and said unto the Lord: Behold, Lord, the half of my goods I give to the poor; and if I have taken any thing from any man by false accusation, I restore *him* fourfold. And Jesus said unto him, This day is salvation come to this house, forsomuch**

> **as he also is a son of Abraham. For the Son of man is come to seek and to save that which was lost.** Luke 19:1-10

You could reason that the difference between the previous rich man and Zacchaeus is that Zacchaeus did <u>not</u> trust in his riches. This is stopping short of the fuller revelation. Having riches and trusting in riches makes it harder to enter the kingdom of God, just as everything else man has and does. The fuller revelation is that everything that man has and everything that man can do falls short (see Rom. 3:23). There is no resource or ability on man's side of the border. It is impossible. Impossible means no power. Man cannot affect the border. Only God can initiate the transaction and cross the border.

Zacchaeus was lost and had a sinner's reputation, but was led to Jesus. Jesus crossed the border and brought salvation. Zacchaeus responded, <u>not</u> offering any works of righteousness, but works of obedience without Jesus asking. Repentance is a manifestation of a new nature (see Acts 3:26). Free will Christians say "No". Everyone has the same opportunity at the border. Zacchaeus crossed the border to Jesus. Zacchaeus acted on the opportunity given him, just as the previous rich man walked away sadly. Thus we have a disputed border crossing. Nevertheless, the border crossing is <u>not</u> disputed with God.

> **For the word of God** *is* **quick, and powerful, and sharper than any twoedged sword, piercing even to the dividing asunder of soul and spirit, and of the joints and marrow, and** *is* **a discerner of the thoughts and intents of the heart.** Heb. 4:12

Here is a sword analogy of the Word preached (see Heb. 4:2). People avoid a sword just as an unregenerate heart avoids God. The piercing of the Word (sword) is God crossing the border to man (see Acts 2:37). Jesus is the Word of God and He is quick or Spiritually alive. He is powerful and has the ability. He is sharp or wise beyond our understanding and He is able to cross the border between the soul and Spirit.

He created the body, down to the joints and marrow. He knows our every thought and our every intent, perhaps because He programmed them in the elect and allowed the prince of this world to program the thoughts of those who perish. Ultimately, man disputes the border, but God knows. The border is crossed when Jesus calls preachers into His harvest to preach the Word and redeem those whom He has chosen (see Luke 10:2). A preacher can speculate that if he or she had said "No" to the call to preach, a whole lot of people would be in hell. Likewise, a whole lot of people will be in heaven due to their "Yes". This is free will speculation. God is limited based upon man's will. I disagree. Those whom He has chosen before the foundation of the world are not dependent upon a preacher's will to say "Yes" to the call to preach or a sinner's will to say "Yes" to Jesus (see Eph. 1:3-5). Jesus will not lose anyone whom the Father has given Him (see John 10:28-29, 17:9-12). His Spirit "makes it happen".

After His Spirit has regenerated his or her heart, the newborn believer will call upon His name. Those who do not believe are judged based upon their works and will perish or be annihilated in a lake of fire after the justice and wrath of God has been satisfied (see Matt. 18:34; John 3:16). Free will Christians see everyone able to cross the border to God based upon his or her choice of God. This creates a playground of mental manipulations and a bit of a circus atmosphere to persuade the unsaved to choose God. Please bear with my folly (see II Cor. 11:1).

- You have the lion jumping through the ring of fire—there is not a hell hot enough for someone who has rejected Christ.

- You have the high wire act with a long distance— eternity is not long enough for someone who has rejected Christ.
- You shoot the target and win a prize— accept Jesus and get ready to experience financial blessings.
- You have your weight guessed— accept Jesus and walk in divine health.
- Swing the hammer and ring the bell— give it a little extra and really mean business when you pray to be saved.

Virtually everything works in the natural world based upon two principles. These are described as a stick and carrot, punishment and rewards, fear and greed, seedtime and harvest, yin and yang, etc. These natural principles are not found in salvation by grace through faith. However, Christians will imply that these natural principles, such as fear, can be used to obtain a Spiritual result. Jesus taught about hell and fear may arise from His words, but fear is not a prerequisite toward salvation. Jesus said to "**Fear not, little flock for it is your Father's good pleasure to give you the kingdom**" (Luke 12:32). Salvation is by grace. Fear is an emotional feeling that encourages a change of behavior or repentance. Repentance is an act that man can do based upon his conscience of right and wrong. Repentance sustains the natural world, but does not win favor toward salvation by grace. Nevertheless, natural principles are often applied in order to obtain Spiritual results or salvation. Today, natural principles are used to persuade a border crossing that is impossible in a Spiritual realm. God controls the Spiritual realm.

Therefore, concerning salvation, Christians dispute the border crossing. Free will Christians try to entice man to "make it happen". Sovereign will Christians trust God to "make it happen". Free will Christians falsely criticize sovereign will Christians about not needing to witness, since God is going to "make it happen". There is no dispute among Christian groups that a disputed border exists concerning salvation and the free will majority has it wrong. In fact, Scripture, church history and contemporary Christianity reveal that the majority often has it wrong.

Concerning Service and Behavior

The border crossing of service and behavior can be transparent to some, while vague to other. Some know exactly what they have been called to do, while others are searching. However, a few general observations can be made.

> **No man can serve two masters: for either he will hate the one, and love the other; or else he will hold to the one, and despise the other. Ye cannot serve God and mammon.** Matt. 6:24

The service and behavior of man fall into two general categories, 1) the Christian and 2) the unsaved.

The Christian:

Paul is an example of a Christian that amplifies and magnifies the grace of God or Holy Spirit's control. Paul's human will is almost non-existent. God crossed the border in order to accomplish His will through Paul. The border is disputed when Paul is looked upon as making these decisions.

> **But by the grace of God I am what I am: and his grace which** *was bestowed* **upon me was not in vain; but I laboured more abundantly than they all: yet not I, but the grace of God which was with me.** I Cor. 15:10

You could reason that Paul could have resisted or chose not to cooperate with the Spirit's control. Paul could have exercised free will. This is the disputed border and can be resolved by understanding sin or missing the mark. Paul was capable of sinning in his natural soul, where the will of man resides. Another definition of free will is the capacity to sin. However, according to Paul, the grace of God was <u>not</u> in vain. He labored in the works of the Lord and it was the Spirit of God that energized and controlled him. This is irresistible grace. Holy Spirit knows the combination that unlocks the human will to do the will of God. God does <u>not</u> have to force His will, just as the owner of a safe does <u>not</u> have to force the door open. He knows the combination. The Potter does <u>not</u> have to force the clay to move, because His hands are able to make it move as He pleases (see Rom. 9:21). Concerning service, Jesus intercedes to the Father and comes into agreement and empowers the Christian led by Holy Spirit to do the greater works that Jesus spoke of.

> **Verily, verily, I say unto you, He that believeth on me, the works that I do shall he do also; and greater *works* than these shall he do; because I go unto my Father.** John 14:12

Most are <u>not</u> personally familiar with sheep today as was common in the first century. Jesus said His sheep know His voice and would follow Him and flee from strangers. We can get bogged down with exceptions and carnal attitudes, but the analogy is valid, even today. However, one of the most difficult periods is waiting on the Lord to lead.

> **And when he putteth forth his own sheep, he goeth before them, and the sheep follow him: for they know his voice. And a stranger will they not follow, but will flee from him: for they know not the voice of strangers.** John 10:4-5

If you understand where the flow comes from, the wait is less difficult. If you believe that you can control the flow, then you can become frustrated as you try to *"make it happen"*.

God will cross the border and enable the Christian to serve Him. This can be vague at times and very transparent at other times (see Isa. 40:31).

The Unsaved:

Even though God has <u>not</u> crossed the border and regenerated the spirit of the unsaved, He can still cross the border and control the consciousness of the unsaved. This is <u>not</u> total continual control, but limited temporal control. After the flood of Noah the Lord made a modification to His creation that prevented the people from building a tower (service) and unity of will (behavior).

> **And the whole earth was of one language, and of one speech. And it came to pass, as they journeyed from the east, that they found a plain in the land of Shinar; and they dwelt there. And they said one to another, Go to, let us make brick, and burn them thoroughly. And they had brick for stone, and slime had they for morter. And they said, Go to, let us build us a city and a tower, whose top** *may reach* **unto heaven; and let us make us a name, lest we be scattered abroad upon the face of the whole earth. And the LORD came down to see the city and the tower, which the children of men builded. And the LORD said, Behold, the people** *is* **one, and they have all one language; and this they begin to do: and now nothing will be restrained from them, which they have imagined to do. Go to, let us go down, and there confound their language, that they may not understand one another's speech. So the LORD scattered them abroad from thence upon the face of all the earth: and they left off to build the city. Therefore**

is the name of it called Babel; because the LORD did there confound the language of all the earth: and from thence did the LORD scatter them abroad upon the face of all the earth. Gen. 11:1-9

Here the consciousness of man was changed to understand a different language. Here we see the negation of the will of the people. The Potter used His power over His clay. God crossed the border to affect the service and behavior of unsaved men (although some may have been saved later). Later in the Old Testament, God sovereignly used other nations to judge His people, Israel.

He turned their heart to hate his people, to deal subtilly with his servants. Ps 105:25

How He does this is vague to understand, but this demonstrates that He can control the behavior of the unsaved (see Jer. 34:22). He does so in order for everyone to know that He is Lord (see Ezek. 32:15). He can control His creation and no one can resist. Does God orchestrate disaster? A disaster is often labeled as an act of God. I am not in the counsel room of God or in the realm of the ruler of disobedience. I do not know. Jesus will work these issues out. I do not try to explain a cause and effort for disaster. Jesus said the sun rises on the evil and on the good and He sends rain on the just and on the unjust (see Matt. 5:45). Some high profile Christian leaders could have avoided apologies when they stated God was sending disaster as judgment. Everyone is called to repent, not understand disaster. Repentance will sustain the earthly culture of both the saved and the unsaved from perishing. Repentance is not a prerequisite for salvation since repentance is something man can do, while salvation is a divine work.

And Jesus answering said unto them, Suppose ye that these Galilaeans were sinners above

all the Galilaeans, because they suffered such things? I tell you, Nay: but, except ye repent, ye shall all likewise perish. Luke 13:2-3

Primarily self and Satan control the masses. Still, God can cross the border to the consciousness of the unsaved and control his or her service and behavior without regenerating the spirit of the unsaved.

Conclusion

Everyone will give an account for his or her words and deeds. Everyone is encouraged to repent in order to sustain the culture. However, God sometimes crosses the border to the consciousness of the unsaved for His own purposes and God always has to cross the border to regenerate the Spirit of His elect. After regeneration or salvation, the Elect do works of repentance due to their new nature, which sustains the earthly culture like salt on the earth (see Matt. 5:13; Jam. 2:26). Both of these border crossings – the conscience of the unsaved and the Spirit of the Elect – are disputed by Christians, but <u>not</u> by God.

Chapter Three

The Analogy of a Robot

An analogy is an object used to represent another object for the purpose of illustration, contrast and teaching. It is <u>not</u> an exact representation. Some analogies in the natural world are appropriate to teach Kingdom truths, while other natural analogies are <u>not</u> (see Matt. 20:25-26). Below are some analogies from Scripture.

Potter and Vessel

Like a Potter shapes clay into a vessel, the Creator has the power to shape people as He wills (see Isa. 64:8; Jer. 18:6; Rom. 9:21). As the clay freely spins around (free will), the Potter places His hand where He will to mold the clay into a vessel. The Potter does <u>not</u> have to force the clay to move. The clay responds. However, a vessel on the potter's wheel has a tendency to shift, just as the will of man does toward sin unless the Potter places His hand on the vessel (see Isa. 63:17). Many reject the analogy of the Potter and exclusively imply that God will <u>never</u> interfere with your right to choose. This book could have been titled "Rare Spiritual Vessels", but vessels are a dated analogy while robotics is a contemporary analogy. <u>Not</u> many vessels are handmade today, while robots are made and used to manufacture many products. A vessel and a robot are similar in that man makes them and both need designing to be beautiful and useful.

What does a robot do? A robot receives instructions and responds. What do Christians do? A Christian should hear and obey God. A comment under Romans 9:21 could state, *"Doesn't the Designer have the ability to program the robot to do a task without making a mistake?"*

Salt

When Jesus said, "**Ye are the salt of the earth,**" do you envision Christians as literal salt (see Matt. 5:13)? Likewise, a robot of Jesus is an analogy, <u>not</u> a literal robot.

Shepherd and Sheep

Jesus described His followers as sheep (see John 10:14). A sheep will usually die without a Shepherd (see Isa. 13:14). Believers are never pictured in Scripture as mighty lions, independent and self-sufficient; rather, they are sheep that are dependent on their Shepherd for His provision and protection.[1] You should <u>not</u> interpret sheep literally. Do you envision sheep in the pulpit, sheep in the choir and sheep in the congregation?

Wind

Jesus used the wind to describe how someone is born of the Spirit (see John 3:8). The main idea is that it is out of man's control. We hear the wind, but we do <u>not</u> know where it comes from or where it is going. Modern science has advanced in knowledge, but only God knows the exact time and location of the wind. The analogy of the wind agrees with the Lord sending out workers into His harvest to preach (see Luke 10:2). Still, no one can be a successful worker in His harvest without His initiative. We would love to have a guaranteed strategy on "how to" have five people born again before lunch and ten after lunch. We would be happy to have a powder to sprinkle into our loved one's drink that would make faith come alive. Likewise, we might like a dial to control the wind, but faith is in the Spiritual realm that God controls.

Eagles

The prophet used eagles and wings to illustrate the continual power and energy from the Lord. Using our own will and power, we become tired and collapse. This is common in ministry and evangelism.

> **But they that wait upon the LORD shall renew** *their* **strength; they shall mount up with wings as eagles; they shall run, and not be weary;** *and* **they shall walk, and not faint.** Isa. 40:31

Vine and Branches

The purpose of this analogy reveals fruit producing substance that flows from the Lord to the disciples, just as nutrients flow from the vine to the branches (see John 15:1-14).

Horticulture

The Lord has established the earth with sowing, growing and reaping. The righteousness and the praise that springs forth is an analogy of this principle.

> **For as the earth bringeth forth her bud, and as the garden causeth the things that are sown in it to spring forth; so the Lord God will cause righteousness and praise to spring forth before all the nations.** Isa. 61:11

Natural man cannot become righteous by self-efforts (see Rom. 10:3-4). Righteousness is due to the infused faith that causes a person to believe and act. Praise and repentance will follow.

Body of Christ

A foot, hand, ear and eye are used in the analogy as individual members (see I Cor. 12:12-27). Jesus is the Head, which controls the body (see Eph. 5:23). This is the closest analogy to the robot of Jesus analogy.

The Robot Analogy

Contemporary analogies are used in sermons and writings to help people understand Scripture during cultural change. A robot is a contemporary analogy. Similar to the above analogies, a robot illustrates the control of God over His creation. Would man make a robot he could <u>not</u> control? Would God make a man He could <u>not</u> control? Some say, "Yes." I say "No" based upon Scripture (see Rom. 9:21; Heb. 10:14-17). If man can control a robot, truly God can do the same with man.

The reasons for the robot analogy are:

- The Designer knows how every part of the robot works.
- The robot analogy isolates the importance of doing the will of the Lord.
- The robot analogy illustrates control from a separate Power.
- A robot is totally obedient, similar to a perfect Christian.
- A robot must be programmed, similar to infused faith and a renewed mind.
- A robot does commands. A Christian does commandments.
- A robot does <u>not</u> expect praise for his actions because he does what is expected.

- A robot does <u>not</u> compare itself to other robots because that would be unwise.
- A robot must be controlled in order to accomplish meaningful tasks.
- A robot is a creation. A Christian is a new creation.

(See Acts 1:8; Matt. 5:48; Rom. 12:2; Luke 17:10; II Cor. 10:12; John 15:5; II Cor. 5:17)

The primary reason against the robot analogy is based upon man using his intellect and will or choosing what to do. However, this is limited to the borders of the natural world. And man is more complex than a robot. Man has a soul where decisions can be made. This can be sin when the mark is missed (see Jam. 5:17). When Holy Spirit is leading, man does <u>not</u> sin (see Rom. 8:2; Gal 5:16-18). The robot analogy is about the nature of God controlling the heart of man.

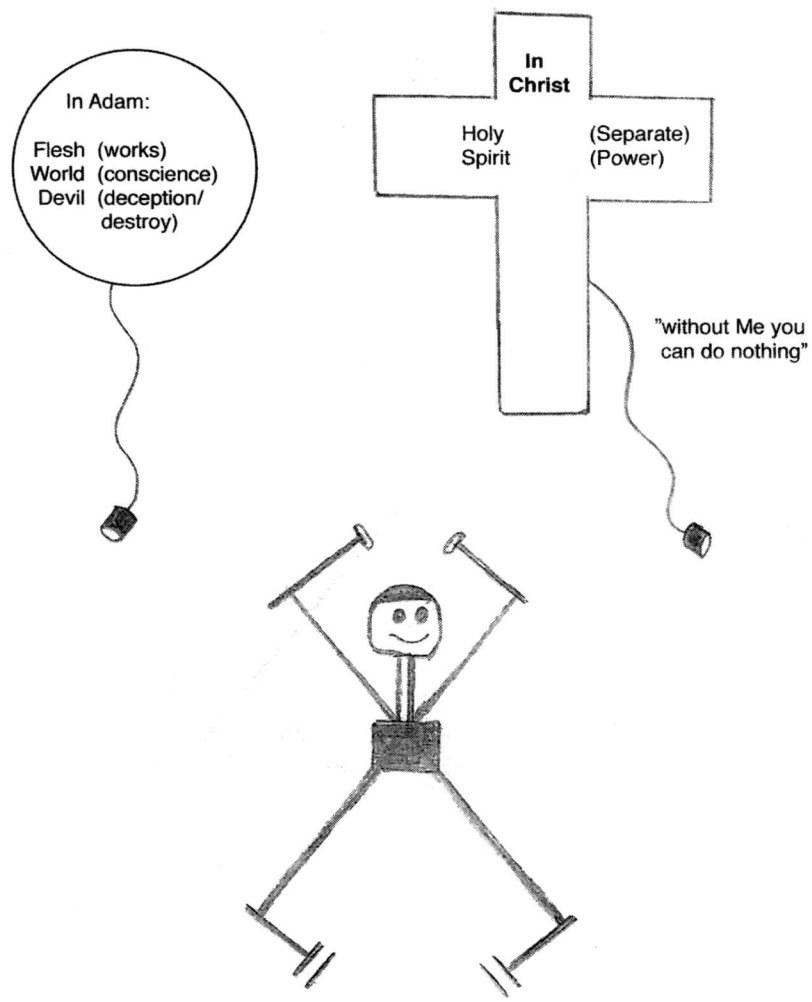

The robot analogy illustrates a vessel unable to do anything without a connection. There is a long list of connections in the Spiritual and physical realm that are beyond man's control (see Ps. 2:3). Only the Designer knows where all fit and how they operate. The Bible identifies the connections. There is a connection that allows the Spirit to come upon a person in the Old Testament and the Spirit to be within a person in the New Testament that empowers the person to do the will of the Lord.

Holy Spirit will glorify Jesus and the individual will have issues with recognition when he knows that Jesus did it. The flesh is about works of self-gratification, while the world operates from the consciousness of man, which can do both good and evil in the natural realm, but is not connected to the Spiritual. Meanwhile, the Devil deceives on one end and destroys on the other. Jesus is superior to these and has come to give life and life more abundantly.

There are two categories, unsaved and saved, that virtually all people fall within. Within these two categories are subcategories. The percentages are speculation based upon Scripture and observation.

1. UNSAVED
   a. Natural People (89%)
   b. Robots of the Flesh (1%)
   c. Robots of Satan (< ½%)

2. SAVED
   a. Disciples (9%)
   b. Robots of Jesus (< 1%)
      i. Activation
      ii. Beautification
      iii. Consummation

Natural People

These people have a conscience and act according to reason. They have the capacity to do good in the natural realm. They can repent and sustain an earthly culture. They create various religions to satisfy their consciences and sustain order. However, they do not understand Spiritual principles. The god of this world may also deceive them, but not totally control them. Natural people will be judged according to their words and deeds.

Robots of the Flesh

Robots of the flesh are without self-control (see II Tim. 3:3). Their behavior is dictated by the five senses of sight, hearing, touch, smell and taste. Natural people can become robots of the flesh due to a lack of intervention from God for an extended amount of time. Sodom and Gomorrah had no remembrance of the judgment of God and became totally corrupt (see Gen. 19; Jude 1:7). When the entire culture becomes robots of the flesh, the culture is unsustainable within the design of creation and ceases to exist.

Robots of Satan

These people are totally controlled by the god of this world. Judas Iscariot and the anti-Christ fall into this subcategory. Consider the past ruler of Tyre and the fall of Satan as describing the same person (see Ezek. 28). It is interesting how some Christians believe that a person can be totally controlled by Satan[2], but not totally controlled by Jesus. Christians acknowledge the sovereignty of God to destroy man, but question the sovereignty of God to fix man. Robots of Satan can have a short life (see Matt. 27:5; John 10:10). Schizophrenia, diagnosed as a splitting of mental functions, could be a period of control by Satan. At judgment day, the robots of Satan would have been better to never been born.

Disciples

Christians are a work in process. A Christian can vacillate to and from a robot of Jesus through discipleship (putting to death the flesh and putting on the Lord Jesus Christ). When you put on the Lord Jesus Christ, you are in a position to hear and obey a command from the Lord, similar to a robot (see Rom. 10:14). Christians can choose to be a disciple, but Christians cannot choose to be a robot of Jesus because Jesus controls the Spiritual realm and He must issue a command (see Acts 8:29, 9:10-16). Meanwhile, the Scriptures testify to being perfect and mature, which is the goal. Perfect and mature Christians act in total obedience to God, but proper interpretation is necessary for Spiritual mindedness. Christians will be rewarded in heaven based upon their obedience and sacrifice.

Activation

Having a Creator who is <u>not</u> involved in time is like having a Creator <u>not</u> involved in creation. During the course of time, the Spirit of God has controlled from heaven a few individuals in order to accomplish His purpose.[3] This is rare, perhaps for just a second of time. The Lord took total control in order to avoid any human failure. This is <u>not</u> seen in Adam and Eve, however Noah was later activated to build an ark (see Gen 6:22). Still later, Jesus activated some fishermen to follow Him. Activation is <u>not</u> contingent upon any type of human yielding, choosing, cooperation, surrendering, repentance, humbling, worship, praise, virtue or any other human initiative or condition. In heaven, these people will cast their crowns back to Jesus because they realize He did it (see Rev. 4:10).

Activation is the ability of the Creator to issue a command to His creation, whether to stop a storm, to speak through a donkey, to feed a prophet using a raven or to stand a man on his feet (see Acts 14:10). Looking at the acts of Adam and Eve (and later Cain and Abel) a case could be made for freedom of will. This is where a broad stroke of freedom can be incorrectly painted that God has given man free will and God will <u>not</u> interfere with man's right to choose. However, God took the acts of Adam, Eve and Cain into account and pronounced judgment. This pattern repeats throughout history. At other times God intervened, such as the tower of Babel, where He confused the tongues (see Gen. 11:9). This is an act by God upon His creation to obtain His purpose without any ability of man to stop, resist, change or avoid. It is like a signal from heaven to do a command, such as speak a different language, similar to a programmer loading new software into a robot. Although the confusion of tongues at the tower of Babel was an act on the consciousness of man, not the Spirit, the principle of activation still applies. The results are absolute. The most familiar act is Spiritual salvation when God installs faith and seals the individual's heart with Holy Spirit.

A future activation will occur in one day with the nation of Israel. God will put His laws in their hearts and they will recognize Jesus, Who they pierced and they will weep for Him (see Jer. 31:33; Rom. 11:26-27; Zech. 12:10). This will fulfill His promises to Israel of a King in David's line during the millennial reign.

The glory of God is a realization that a marvelous work has occurred that only God was able to accomplish (see Dan. 3:25-28). The Lord actively took control. The activation may be immediate or delayed based upon the discretion of the Lord. This is observed in Enoch, when "**God took him**" and when the disciples left their fishing nets and immediately followed Jesus (see Gen. 5:24; Matt. 5:20). Meanwhile, a brief delay is seen in the call of Moses to return to Egypt (see Exod. 4). A longer delay is seen in the call of the prophet Jonah to preach to the Gentile nation of Assyria (see Jonah). The Lord activates as He wills, sometimes immediately, sometimes with delays. The timing is always perfect to match His nature and the targeted human personality. Therefore, we do not have a death certificate for Enoch. The disciples became fishers of men. Moses went to Egypt and Jonah preached in Assyria. The Lord controls people without force to accomplish His will, even Spiritual salvation (see Eph. 1).

Beautification

A disciple can place himself in a position to be a robot of Jesus by reaching a mature and perfect state. A disciple's faith can reach a level that is pleasing or beautiful to the Lord.[4] However, you can be in the will of God and never reach this level of discipleship based upon your individual gift(s) and calling. Beautification is the shaping of a disciple into a perfect vessel. This is the purpose of Scripture of which I encourage for further explanation (see Isa. 52:1; II Tim. 3:16-17; I John 2:5). Scripture renews the mind and the disciple can know the good will of God. The disciple can continue renewing his or her mind and know the acceptable will of God. Finally, the disciple can advance to the perfect or robotic will of God (see Rom. 12:2).

Jesus is the Word of God and our example of beautification (see John 13:15). Jesus glorified the Father by doing His will while on the earth (see John 17:4). Then, Jesus prayed that His followers would be brought to perfection (see John 17:23). No limitations should be placed on the ability of the Lord to accomplish His purpose with His creation.

> *Even* **every one that is called by my name: for I have created him for my glory, I have formed him; yea, I have made him.** Isa. 43:7

Jesus was human in order to represent mortal man on the cross. The Name of Jesus is unique and special to man. Jesus is the only Name of God that is also the Name of a Man and therefore the door for man to enter the kingdom of God. The parts fit. A match is found. Jesus had a human mind and a human will (see Phil. 2:7). He denied His human will in order to obey His Father (see Matt. 26:39). Obedience to His Father was paramount (see John 4:34, 6:38).[5] Jesus' ultimate act of obedience was death on the cross (see Phil. 2:8). The Father orchestrated His Son's death by placing the actors on the scene. One was filled by Satan to betray Him. Another was told, "**he would have no power at all unless it was given to him from above**" (see John 19:11).

Now Jesus is the Author and Finisher of our faith (see Heb. 12:2). He asks us to deny our human will and follow Him (see Phil. 2:5). Our obedience to take up our cross may require death (see Matt. 16:24). Virtually, no one desires to die, so God changes the nature of a person to desire to do His will by seeing the resurrection in the future (see II Cor. 5:17; Heb. 11:19). Holy Spirit within the Christian harmonizes with the will of God. God does <u>not</u> force[6] His will, but the enemy may force his will on the follower to disobey God. The follower should obey God even when the enemy threatens with death. The glory of God is to control someone by faith without force. Force is <u>not</u> needed because the heart is enlightened to the power of the resurrection and future life in a heavenly city. They are obedient to the faith implanted by God (see Rom. 1:5, 16:26-27). It is impressive when God is able to do this. In opposition, free will gives vainglory to man. Jesus said that <u>not</u> everyone that calls Him "**Lord, Lord**" would enter the kingdom of heaven but only those who do the will of the Father in heaven (see Matt. 7:21). In beautification, reading your Bible and prayer become more joyful than fellowshipping with your best friend on earth (see John 21:15).

Further explanation is in the Scripture. The Word of God creates a wall between the old man with its corrupt soulish nature and the new Spiritual man (see Heb. 4:12). Soulish implies the self-seeking and the self-pleasing nature of man. Meanwhile, the Word is Spiritual and Self-giving. When you put on the Lord Jesus Christ (or think Spiritual thoughts from the Word), the Spiritual man is nourished and the flesh is denied (see Eph. 4:22). Jesus has redeemed the sinful soul of man, but the new man must walk in the new nature (see Rom 6:6). The Lord is long-suffering during this process, although the soulish nature prefers to shorten or avoid the process (see II Pet. 3:9).

> **And be not conformed to this world: but be ye transformed by the renewing of your mind, that ye may prove what *is* that good, and acceptable, and perfect, will of God. Rom. 12:2**

Beautification is the results of this process. The new nature led by Holy Spirit, without the old man or human mind being engaged, reacts to the will of the Father. This is robotic. The robot analogy could be used as a ruler to examine obedience: robotic obedience on the highest and a sin unto death on the lowest. Robotic obedience is <u>not</u> a 24/7 occurrence. Robotic obedience is rare due to the struggle between the Spirit and the flesh (see Gal. 5:17). It is a daily declaration (see Matt. 6:10).

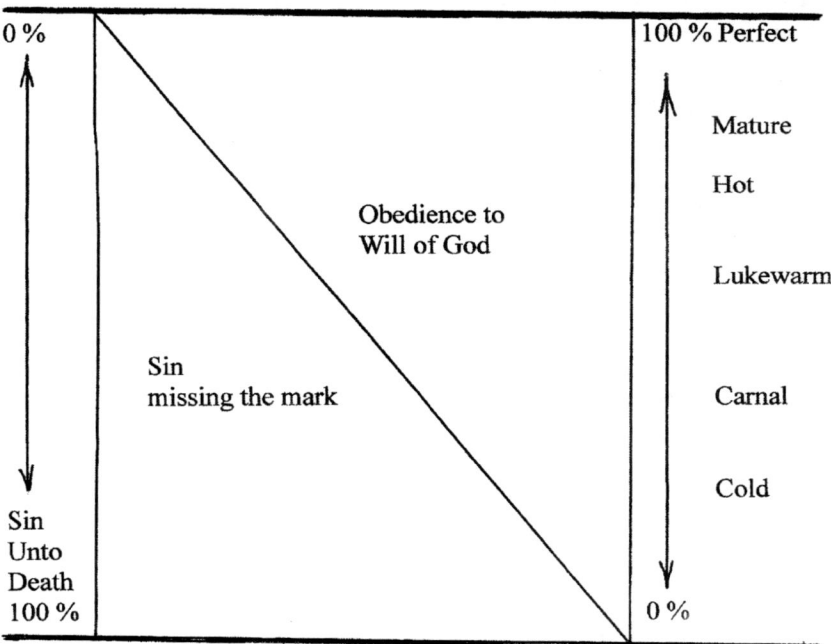

Christians have the nature of God in the Person of Holy Spirit. Holy Spirit cannot sin or miss the mark (see I John 3:9). Therefore Jesus can expect a high level of obedience.

Be perfect, therefore, as your heavenly Father is perfect. Matt. 5:48

If you imply that total obedience is possible, like a robotic action, immediately questions arise because the mind is being renewed from this world's principles to the Spiritual's world principles (see Rom. 12:2). I have heard two pastors preach, "*God does not make robots.*" One added the common reasoning, "*God will honor your right to choose.*" This is a principle of the world. Self-will testifies to the unjust (see I Pet. 2:10). On the contrary— the Potter does have power over the clay and the sheep will follow their Shepherd (see Rom. 9:21; John 10:4). Will the Shepherd let the sheep choose to wander off and do his or her selfish will? Yes, to a limited degree, but not completely.

This is not legalism. Legalism is trying to harmonize the corrupt soul with the holy law. Grace is God-given faith and Holy Spirit power to speak and act the will of God. Under grace, the Spiritual man delights in the law of God (see Ps. 1:2; Rom. 7:22). This is discipleship. You might ask, "*How can these things be?*" It involved putting to death the deeds of the flesh and the carnal mind that cannot please God. Death means separation. Death means that it no longer operates and control is taken over by the Spirit (see Rom. 8:5-14). You are not making choices or decisions in your carnal mind. Jesus taught to not take any thought concerning carnal matters (see Matt. 6:25-34). This may occur for .0165 seconds in your entire Christian life or it may be more regular. Thoughts are part of the living soul obtained from God (see Gen. 2:7). However, thoughts were corrupted from the evil portion of the fruit of the tree of the knowledge of good and evil (see Gen. 3:7).

Therefore the mind needs transforming into a Spiritual mind, loaded with the Word of God (see Rom. 12:2). A diligent disciple will continue in the Word until he or she is made free from the false signals that come from the corrupt nature that is in bondage to sin (see John 8:31-32). Christians are free from sin, but the carnal mind thinks incorrectly and needs reprogramming with the Truth (Word) of this freedom (see Rom. 6). Freedom from sin leans toward obeying God like a mechanical robot. Meanwhile, making choices in the natural realm with a corrupt soul is like a defective robot with a weak battery. An unsaved person making a choice in the Spiritual realm is like a defective robot with a dead battery (see Eph. 2:1).

The Analogy of a Robot

What is a robot of Jesus? There is no one definition of robot which satisfies everyone and many people have their own.[7] Here is my definition: *A robot of Jesus is a chosen vessel of God when controlled by Holy Spirit demonstrates obedience in thought (Isa. 55:8; II Cor. 10:5), word (Jer. 20:9; Matt. 10:20) and deed (Acts 26:9; Rom. 15:18). The chosen vessel has regressive and progressive stages in time that reach fruition (transformation by the Lord, <u>not</u> self) at the end of time.* Do you have the ability to be a mindless robot? This big idea – that much of our everyday thinking, feeling and acting operates outside our conscious awareness – "is a difficult one for people to accept," reports New York University psychologists John Bargh and Tanya Chartrand (1999). We are understandably biased to believe that our own intentions and deliberate choices rule our lives.[8] Butch Trucks, one of the drummers for the Allman Brothers Band described what the band calls "*hittin the note.*" Notice what he says about the activity of the brain which sounds like robotic activity with the brain disengaged.

> "Hittin the note is reaching that point where you can't do any wrong", said Butch. "With us, when we're playing music it's where the brain goes away and the body just does what it's supposed to do, and there's no thought and there's no question, and no matter what you do, it's right. It's getting to that spiritual level where the communication is total, but it's <u>not</u> mental."[9]

"Hittin the note" is similar to hitting the mark or obedience to God. Scripture encourages perfection, which is the opposite of missing the mark or sin (see Matt. 5:48; II Cor. 7:1; II Tim. 3:17). In a Christian realm this mindless possibility exists as Dietrich Bonhoeffer wrote: "*Christ's virtue, the virtue of discipleship, can only be accomplished so long as you are entirely unconscious of what you are doing.*"[10] In order to do the will of God, mental activity is <u>not</u> required (see Luke 12:11). This is

<u>not</u> a broad-brush stroke, but a narrow-brush stroke of robotic activity. This is rare. This is Spiritual. Yet even when the brain is engaged, the capacity for obedience exists.

> **Casting down imaginations, and every high thing that exalteth itself against the knowledge of God, and bringing into captivity every thought to the obedience of Christ;** II Cor. 10:5

The Scripture states, "**For to be carnally minded is death, but to be Spiritual minded is life and peace**" (Rom 8:6). Do <u>not</u> take complete obedience off the table. Avoid the limitations of today's philosophy that states, "*God does <u>not</u> make robots.*" Paul encouraged a mindset like Christ Jesus. The high point includes equality with God (see Phil. 2:5-6). Meanwhile, the range of obedience may include physical death (see Phil. 2:8; Rev. 12:11). However, Holy Spirit is sealed in hearts and Christians are <u>not</u> lacking (see Eph. 1:13). Therefore in beautification, you can be Spiritual minded and act in obedience or led by Holy Spirit without the natural mind being engaged.

Consummation

At the end of time, Christians will be transformed to immortal beings and be like Jesus — obedient in thought, word and deed. Consummation is a recipe with ingredients, instructions and transformation to make a robot of Jesus.

Ingredients for a robot of Jesus:

- Temporal existence in time
- Dust of the ground
- Breath of life
- Fall of man
- Redemption
- Holy Spirit
- Discipleship

- Physical Death
- Mortality to immortality
- Tree of Life

Instructions for a robot of Jesus:

Caution — do <u>not</u> attempt this yourself. God performs these instructions. Except for discipleship, it is impossible for man to do them (see Matt. 19:26).

In the beginning God created the heaven and the earth. Gen. 1:1

"**In the beginning**" was the creation of the ingredient of time. It is important to understand that time has a beginning and an end. Time is a temporary ingredient that allows change to occur. That is why God cannot change because He is outside the realm of time. At the end of time, eternity does <u>not</u> start. Eternity has connotations with time and is a concept of man's reasoning. If time were permanent, there would <u>not</u> be a last day (see John 6:39). We are <u>not</u> able to understand or have <u>not</u> been given the revelation of life outside the realm of time. However, the Christian uses time on earth to test, exercise and strengthen his or her faith, which glories the Creator. Obviously, time is <u>not</u> a faithful friend to the physical body. A visual of sin can be observed by placing a picture of a newborn baby beside a picture of a retiring Hollywood movie actor or actress. Beautiful people age and are set on the shelf. Jesus never ages. He looks the same yesterday, today and always (see Heb. 13:8).

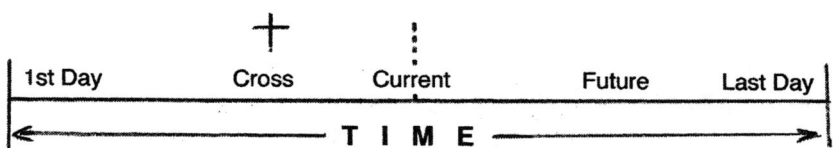

From the dust of the ground the Lord formed man and breathed into his nostrils the breath of life. Next, the Lord fashioned woman from the man. Adam and Eve were the starting or beginning point. God said let us make man in our image[11], but the full splendor of the image will appear later at the end of time (see I Cor. 15:46-49). Suppose you tell the family, *"Let us make a cake."* The starting point is when you crack an egg in a bowl. Adam and Eve were not the final image, just as the egg is only one ingredient for the cake. Adam and Eve were the starting point, like two eggs cracked in a bowl. The fall of man was part of the recipe, but the final image will appear when we see Jesus, just as the cake appears after baking and the icing.

> **And God said, Let us make man in our image, after our likeness:** Gen. 1:26a

God is One with three manifestations of the same God.

> Father
> Son
> Holy Spirit

"Trinity" is an awkward theological word that identifies the three manifestations (Father, Son and Holy Spirit) of One God. Generally speaking, the Father is the will of God, while Jesus, the Son, is the Word of God, while Holy Spirit is the active arm of God (see Matt. 6:9-10; John 1:14; Acts 1:8).

The anatomy of man consist of three parts:

> Spirit – Christians live by faith of the Spirit (see II Cor. 4:13, 5:7). The Christian should not be conformed to this world and wrestles with spiritual wickedness in high places (see Rom. 12:2; Eph. 6:13). The disobedient live by the spirit of this world, according to the course of this world,

according to the prince of the power of the air (see I Cor. 2:12; Eph. 2:2).

Soul – The intellect, emotion and will of man. The Lord can control the soul, but encourages repentance. Holy Spirit harmonizes with godly repentance. Within the soul a conscience to know right and wrong exists. The disobedient are in bondage and dead to sin (see Eph. 2:1,5).

Body – The physical and visible part of man where the invisible soul and Spirit reside until separation at death.

Jesus provided the ingredient of redemption from the bondage of sin. Jesus said from the cross, "**It is finished**". Redemption is complete. Jesus died for the sins from the corrupt soul of man. Now, the redeemed have the nature of God with the gift of Holy Spirit and their names are written in heaven.

Transformation:

Unless taken in the rapture, physical death will occur (see I Thes. 4:17). Then the mortal will be transformed into an immortal vessel sustained from the tree of life. The old man (nature) will be transformed (see I Cor. 15:44). Christians will be in the image of Jesus and fulfill the Word spoken, "**Let us make man in our image**" (Gen. 1:26a). The full splendor of His image was the intent of God when He spoke, "**Let us make man in our image.**" The fallen sinful nature of Adam and Eve was the starting point and only one ingredient toward the image.

> **Beloved, now are we the sons of God, and it doth not yet appear what we shall be: but we know that, when he shall appear, we shall**

> **be like him; for we shall see him as he is.**
> I John 3:2

The Lord will reign. Robotic obedience will occur. Missing the mark (sin) will <u>not</u>.

> **And the seventh angel sounded; and there were great voices in heaven, saying, The kingdoms of this world are become the kingdoms of our Lord, and of his Christ; and he shall reign for ever and ever.** Rev. 11:15

If the will of God is done in heaven, which is our final abode, we will be doing the will of God in heaven. We will <u>not</u> be in the image of a robot or an exact representation of a robot, but we will be similar, void of an independent or self-will and full of the joy of obedience. Until that transformation, faith, hope and love abide (see I Cor. 13:13).

Faith

The Lord asked man to seek Him. The Lord commanded man to obey Him. The Lord pleaded with man to respect his neighbor. The Lord exhorted man to live in accordance with His plans. Yet the only means to accomplish this was through faith. Faith comes to man from God as an added endowment (see Gal. 3:23). Faith is a gift paid for by Jesus (see Eph. 2:8). Faith enables obedience to the will of the Father, which is righteous living. It is easy to tell someone to just believe in Jesus, but unless the substance of faith drops down from heaven into his or her heart, they will remain the same.

> **Now faith is the substance of things hoped for, the evidence of things not seen.** Heb. 11:1

The Greek word "hypostasis", translated "**substance**" in the Scripture above is the same Greek word that describes

Jesus as the "**Person**" (see Heb. 1:3). The essence of Jesus is faith (see II Thes. 3:3). Faith is <u>not</u> a natural substance within man (see Rom. 10:17). Faith is the Word, the will and the ability of God infused into the heart of man (see Rom. 12:2; Heb. 11:1-3). The apostles knew where faith came from and Who controlled faith.

> **And the apostles said unto the Lord, Increase our faith.** Luke 17:5

The robot analogy is an aid toward understanding faith. Just as a robot cannot operate in the natural realm without an electrical current, man cannot operate in the Spiritual realm without faith (see Jam. 2:26). Faith is the invisible substance that flows from God that enables man to know and do.

The writer of Hebrews 11 examines all three categories of the robot analogy (activation, beautification and consummation). Hebrews 11 is <u>not</u> the hall of fame, heroes of the faith chapter of the Bible, but the glory of God chapter. God infused faith into these individuals as example of His ability to control. Man does <u>not</u> put his faith in God, but God puts His substance of faith in man. With faith, God makes perfect children (Heb. 11:40). By faith, God created the universe and by faith man is enabled to act according to God's will. Faith is an attribute of God that enables man to act contrary to self and contrary to the principles of this present world. Faith sees a place whose Builder and Maker is God (consummation). Faith is <u>not</u> a human attribute (see I Pet. 1:5). Faith comes to man by hearing the Word of God (beautification) or instantaneous (activation). Scripture reveals human nature as unfaithful and unbelieving (see Gen. 3-Rev. 20). Therefore, one should examine self and <u>not</u> criticize the failures in others. When man is faithful and believing, it is due to the faith received from God.

> **But without faith** *it is* **impossible to please** *him*: **for he that cometh to God must believe**

that he is, and *that* **he is a rewarder of them that diligently seek him.** Heb 11:6

A disciple can become pleasing or beautify to God by denying self. Self looks at the natural world with natural senses. The mind can wander and dwell on worldly matters. The mind can entertain the past or dread the future. The heart can desire the things of this world or harbor resentment toward others. Instead, a better usage of time is to seek the Lord (see Mark 9:29). The reward is faith. Faith reveals His will and enables man to act. **Hope** is an attribute of man (see Acts 17:27, 24:15). Hope remained after the fall of Adam. Man can hope, but faith comes from God, giving revelations and creating miracles, including salvation. Hope is opening your hand and faith is the substance God places in your hand. An example of faith coming to someone who hoped to get well is the woman with an issue of blood. This woman did not have faith until the virtue of faith from Jesus passed into her. Otherwise, if she had faith, she would not have needed Jesus.

And a woman having an issue of blood twelve years, which had spent all her living upon physicians, neither could be healed of any, Came behind *him*, **and touched the border of his garment: and immediately her issue of blood stanched. And Jesus said, Who touched me? When all denied, Peter and they that were with him said, Master, the multitude throng thee and press** *thee*, **and sayest thou, Who touched me? And Jesus said, Somebody hath touched me: for I perceive that virtue is gone out of me. And when the woman saw that she was not hid, she came trembling, and falling down before him, she declared unto him before all the people for what cause she had touched him, and how she was healed immediately.**

And he said unto her, Daughter, be of good comfort: thy faith hath made thee whole; go in peace. Luke 8:43-48

She came with hope and left with faith. Jesus declared that her faith had made her whole, but the faith or ability to heal came from Jesus – the faith that became hers, <u>not</u> faith that she mustered up. Whenever Jesus recognized someone's faith, that faith came from God, either by hearing the Word, prayer or hoping to receive. Hearing, prayer and hope are human, but faith to believe is a divine attribute. (*This is pounding on some hard concrete in the theological world where faith is recognized as a human attribute.*) Believing that faith comes from within man is feeding on the bottom. Jesus criticized His disciples for <u>not</u> having faith to cast out a mute and deaf spirit. When the disciples asked Jesus to explain, Jesus stated that prayer was needed (see Mark 9:18-29). Therefore, faith can be obtained through prayer. Lifting up holy hands toward God in prayer is similar to robotic antennas in the Spiritual realm (see I Tim. 2:8). When a miracle happens, you should turn around and give Jesus the glory for giving you the faith.

And his name through faith in his name hath made this man strong, whom ye see and know: yea, the faith which is by <u>Him</u> hath given <u>him</u> this perfect soundness in the presence of you all. Acts 3:16

In the Name of Jesus, Peter and John healed a lame man (see Acts 3). In the Scripture above, the two occurrences of the pronoun "H**im**" are underlined. The first occurrence I have capitalized because I believe Jesus is the Reference, <u>not</u> the man that was healed. Faith passed from the Name of Jesus to the lame man in order to accomplish the healing. Faith is the DNA code of God. Faith is like rain from heaven to sustain Spiritual life on earth. Like wiretapping into a terrorist's conversation to avoid a catastrophe; faith is a revelation from heaven that avoids corruption from the lusts of this world (see II Pet. 1:4). The Lord controls the distribution of faith and once received, that faith becomes the individual's gift in order to do His will (see Mark 11:24). This should not be difficult to understand since the physical body and the invisible soul is a creation of God, just as the invisible enablement of faith is a gift imparted into the heart of man. You did not create your body and soul. These natural attributes came from God, just as the Spiritual substance of faith comes from God.

1) Natural Attributes
   a. Sight
   b. Hearing
   c. Touch
   d. Smell
   e. Taste
2) Transitional Attribute – mind should be renewed with Word of Faith
3) Spiritual Attribute of Faith

There are Scriptures that appear to recognize faith as a human attribute, but I do not find Scripture where man is able to muster up faith independent of God. God is always near when the individual's faith is recognized because God infused the faith into the individual.

Nevertheless, it does not end there. The purpose of this life is to test and exercise the infused faith in order to accomplish the Author's objectives. This can be praise at the Author's coming or joy after enduring (see I Pet. 1:7; Jam. 5:11).

Love

God is love (see I John 4:8). Love is an attribute of God illustrated to the highest level by Jesus suffering for others (see John 15:13). Love is obedience to God (see John 14:15; I Cor. 13:5a). Can a robot love? No. Can a sinful human being love God? No, the carnal mind is enmity against God (see

Rom 8:7). We love Him because He first loved us and placed Holy Spirit within us so that we might love. We love because the nature of God is within our hearts (see I Tim. 1:14).

> **Jesus said unto him, Thou shalt love the Lord thy God with all thy heart, and with all thy soul, and with all thy mind. This is the first and great commandment.** Matt. 22:37-38

In order to love at this level, with all your heart, soul and mind, Holy Spirit must control you. Love is obedience or you put the power current to love by obedience. This is a mature, perfect Christian. Meanwhile, fear is a byproduct of disobedience (see Gen. 3:10). Obedience leaves no room for fear to exist (see I John 4:18).

The robot analogy helps understand the power and control from God. This is *not* about what you are doing with your life, getting fully committed or making Jesus the Lord of your life. This is *not* about doing, committing, making, choosing, deciding or getting dedicated. These are all human attempts to upgrade the corrupt soul inherited from Adam. The robot analogy is about the life of Jesus flowing into you. Some call it *"the anointing"* or *"Holy Ghost revival"*; others might call it *"operating in the gifts of the Spirit"*. Others prefer *"Christian Perfection"*. The apostle Paul wrote, **"Walk not after the flesh, but after the Spirit"** (see Rom. 8:4). The robotics of love consists of:

- Doing His commands (see John 15:10)
- Never failing
- Never thinking evil
- Kindness
- Longsuffering
- No envy
- No self-seeking
- Never behave unseemly (see I Cor. 13:4-8).

The robot analogy is birthed from a concern to avoid hampering Spiritual growth. The emphasis is placed on obedience instead of the failure of man. This is not legalism, but a love of God and people (see Eph. 5:1-2). Legalism is trying to act righteous by self-efforts from the corrupt nature. Instead, the corrupt nature should be denied and put to death where it no longer operates. Love is obedience due to a new nature. Scripture encourages an evolution toward a robotic obedience by growing in the grace and knowledge of the Lord Jesus and renewing the mind with the Word of God. Ultimately one comes to the place where he or she is led and controlled by Holy Spirit, where Jesus can load new upgraded commands.

> **A new commandment I give unto you, That ye love one another; as I have loved you, that ye also love one another.** John 13:34

Instead we often hear of ourselves as free moral agents who control our own destiny by our choices. Man does have a human will, but God has given Holy Spirit to do His will. Obeying His commandments is the evidence of a love for God and status as a member of the family of God.

However, a robot cannot hope. Hope does not fit in the robot analogy, but faith and love do. Faith is the software and love is the power that works within the parameters of the Creator. Faith is the intelligence and nature of the Designer. Love is discipline to respond in obedience. Perfection is the result that gives glory to the Creator.

Criticism

> **Hath not the potter power over the clay, of the same lump to make one vessel unto honour, and another unto dishonour?** Rom. 9:21

Free will advocates brush over the analogy of a vessel made by a Potter in relationship to the shaping of a person's nature and destiny. Likewise, brushing over the robot analogy is expected. One fine Christian lady said she disagreed with me 100%. This is the culture we live in. The majority of the American Christian church is Arminian or free will, meaning, "*You chose.*" Meanwhile, the indigenous American philosophy is pragmatism, meaning, "*Whatever works*". This is a land where the awards of human accomplishments surround us. Concerning accomplishments for the Kingdom of God, virtually nothing is accomplished by the will of man, some things are accomplished by the co-operation of God and man, but great things are accomplished by robotic obedience to Holy Spirit. Meanwhile, the American constitution grants freedom. I love my country, but I prefer the Kingdom of God. The robot analogy may seem like a violation of one's civil rights or a crime of kidnapping by taking someone against his or her will. Meanwhile, the mantra of the Christian church is praise for God, but the praise of man is often the reality (see Mark 7:6-7). Therefore "free will" theology dominates the American church while freedom and pragmatism dominate our country. Within this culture the robot analogy can seem absurd like — you are out of your mind (see Acts 26:14). No, instead it is a Spiritual mind that loves or obeys the Lord with all their heart and with all their soul and with all their mind (see Deut. 6:5; Matt. 22:27; John 14:15).

Conclusion

Here is reality. The Head of the church is Jesus and the government shall be upon His shoulders. Right now, the Father is in heaven with Jesus on His right hand. The world is His footstool. He controls at times and He relaxes at times. Everything and everyone is at His discretion. Holy Spirit abides in Christians. Growing in the grace and knowledge of the Lord Jesus Christ is transitioning from making choices with the corrupt soul inherited from Adam, toward knowing His will, hearing His commands and doing them. Christians testify to this control. One said Holy Spirit would <u>not</u> allow him to reply to a lady that said something about Jesus that he disagreed with. This is obedience in word. Another said that God would not allow him to remove some questionable religious material from a hotel he was staying at. This is obedience in deed.

Christian life in this world is a struggle with the nature of Adam and Holy Spirit, but God communicates with His Word and His Spirit. To state that God does not make robots, hints that Christians cannot win this struggle. The robot analogy may appear extreme, but free will appears extreme when you study the Bible. There is a will of God for every moment. **Wherefore be ye not unwise, but understanding what the will of the Lord is** (Eph. 5:17). We should be able to know when to turn the television off, where to park our car, where and what to buy, what type and how much food to eat, etc. We should be able to know the will of the Lord by renewing our minds and prayer. Therefore, being led by Holy Spirit and obeying God is possible. It is possible to be a robot of Jesus.

Chapter Four
Old Testament Robots

History could be described as a great painting with wide contrasts of good and evil brush strokes that illustrate the purpose of the Almighty in saving mankind from a destructive fallen nature. History verifies the truth that disobedience to God results in death (see Gen. 2:17). History rebukes the lie that man shall be as gods (see Gen. 3:5; Acts 12:22-23)).

The Lord wrote a song. He used every range on the musical scale with the most pleasant harmony to sound the greatest blessing and the sourest discord to noise the worst curse (see Deut. 28). Then He played the song with the nation of Israel as an instrument for the world to hear. He hit every note of the law to bless and every note of the law to curse. Then He sat back to wait for the applause, but the people's ears were dull of hearing (see Isa. 6:9; Micah 7:16).

> **If ye be willing and obedient, ye shall eat the good of the land: but if ye refuse and rebel, ye shall be devoured with the sword: for the mouth of the Lord hath spoken** it. Isa. 1:19-20

The Lord is frugal. He prefers man to repent using the conscience that He has given man. When man does not repent, He either judges or shows mercy. His judgment results in destruction (see Gen. 6:13, 19:13). His mercy results in kindness (see Jonah 4). Thus time moves forward with judgment and mercy.

Obedience to God in the Old Testament resulted in a stable prosperous nation on earth where the people enjoyed the good of the land, not entrance into the Kingdom of God. The Old Testament covenants provided every opportunity for man to obey God and at the same time exhausted every possibility of man possessing the ability to obey God (see Gen. 3:1-Mal. 4:6). The Holy law and the natural soul of man do not relate (see Hosea 8:12). His Spirit was needed (see Jud. 3:10). Faith was needed (see Deut. 32:20). Man does not obey God by sight. Man can see miraculous acts of God that bring favor and victory. Still, human nature is lacking the ability to follow the Holy law of God (see Deut. 29:2-4).

However, those chosen and anointed with Holy Spirit will inherit the Kingdom of God (see Ps. 23:6; Heb. 11). When the Old Testament leader had the Spirit of God or the anointing, the people had a chance (see Jud. 2:7-13). In the Old Testament, only certain individuals were anointed by Holy Spirit (see Isa. 63:11). Therefore, the possibility of a high level of obedience was limited to a few. Nevertheless, at times the people rejected their anointed leader, whether prophet, priest or king. At other times, they cherished their anointed leader. The soul of man is able to choose, but without Holy Spirit, the flesh virtually always yields the upper hand (see Deut. 30:19, 31:29; Jud. 2:17).

Then said he, These are the two anointed ones, that stand by the Lord of the whole earth. Zech. 4:14

Therefore, when reading the Old Testament, it is important to find and understand what God is doing, rather than credit or condemn man for his behavior. It is easy to get caught up in feelings and give someone a bit of praise before looking at the Source of his or her obedience. You could discover a rare Spiritual robot of Jesus.

Noah

In the days of Noah, the soul of man had progressively tilted toward corruption. No one had a reference of a good decision. The imagination of man's heart was evil from his youth (see Gen. 8:21). Therefore the Spirit of God was needed in order for man to know and obey God. Without the Spirit of God, the whole population was corrupt, including Noah. This shows total depravity of man to obey God and sustain an earthly existence.

> **And God saw that the wickedness of man** *was* **great in the earth, and** *that* **every imagination of the thoughts of his heart** *was* **only evil continually.** Gen. 6:5

> **But Noah found grace in the eyes of the Lord.** Gen. 6:8

Noah found unmerited favor because Noah had an evil heart. Noah was no different from the whole population in his inability to obey God; otherwise, Noah would have merited favor from God. The favor would have been based on something in Noah and grace would not have been needed. Grace is not based on merit (see Rom. 11:5-6). Grace is a bestowal of favor based upon a decision by God that is beyond our ability to know why the favor was given.

After grace, Noah became a man of faith and a preacher of righteousness. This was a transformation by God. Noah is often given credit for being a righteous vessel that God recognized. If so, grace was not needed. If the favor of God is contingent upon man, grace does not exist. Noah became righteous by an act of grace that saved his family and mankind from destruction.

Abraham

God improved man through the pattern of faith that was perfected in Abraham, so much so, that regenerated man is called a new man (see II Cor. 5:17; Eph. 2:15, 4:24; Col 3:9-10; Heb. 10:14-16). The old man was painstakingly proven faulty and unable to attain the high standards of God (see Gen. 6:5-7). The robot analogy applies to Abraham. God spoke perfection into Abraham.

> **And when Abram was ninety years old and nine, the Lord appeared to Abram, and said unto him, I *am* the Almighty God; walk before me, and be thou perfect.** Gen. 17:1

The work that the Lord did on Abraham is incredible. God gave Abraham faith (see Rom. 4:9). Abraham saw things in the future and did <u>not</u> hesitate to sacrifice his own son because of his vision of the resurrection (see John 8:56; Heb. 11:17-19). This gave glory to God for implanting faith into Abraham to act in obedience (see Rom. 4:20). Initially, Abraham had only flesh and soul. He could <u>not</u> believe without God imputing faith in him (see Rom 4:1-2).

Imagine the most difficult task a robot might do. Imagine building a robot to travel around the world, through land and sea without the battery going dead and capture photographs of evil acts in order to expose and suppress them. Abraham was given the most difficult task of sacrificing Isaac. When Abraham lifted the knife, the Lord knew that He had perfected faith within the heart of a man and future redemption through faith would be successful (see Gen. 22:10-18; Gal. 4:28). Abraham is the father of faith, the seed implanted into God's children (see Rom. 4:11; Heb. 11:1).

Job

After faith was perfected in Abraham, God took the same substance of faith and placed it into Job in order to flaunt Satan (see Job 1:8). The book of Job is insightful in Spiritual warfare. The Lord did something Spiritual to Job by placing a hedge around him and something Spiritual within Job by divine impartation (faith).

> **There was a man in the land of Uz, whose name** *was* **Job; and that man was perfect and upright, and one that feared God, and eschewed evil.** Job 1:1

There is nothing good within the human heart in its natural fallen state. The righteous or just live by faith (see Hab. 2:4; Rom 1:17). To be righteous, Job was implanted with Spiritual traits. Then the Lord withdrew His protection and Job's faith was tested. Job lost his children, livestock and health. He was left with his wife, land, a troubled life and the capacity for obedience. Job's choices did not determine his miserable destiny. Instead, Job's destiny was established from a discussion between God and Satan (see Job 1-2). Later, he was troubled in his soul by the false accusations from his friends. Job's friends compared obedience with blessings and sin with hardships. Job disagreed and offered examples of prosperous wicked men. Job words were meaningless to his friends. They were locked into their simplistic analysis. They were cemented in tradition and contemporary religion. Still, Job stands firm in his faith and waits. The Lord confirms Job's words. Before his faith was depleted the Lord appeared and reinstated Job. Before Job's faith was exhausted, Job was filled again. Job is an example of obedience in thought, word and deed, perhaps even, robotic obedience.

> **In all this Job sinned not, nor charged God foolishly.** Job 1:22

> **And it was *so*, that after the LORD had spoken these words unto Job, the LORD said to Eliphaz the Temanite, My wrath is kindled against thee, and against thy two friends: for ye have not spoken of me** the thing that is **right, as my servant Job** hath**. Therefore take unto you now seven bullocks and seven rams, and go to my servant Job, and offer up for yourselves a burnt offering; and my servant Job shall pray for you: for him will I accept: lest I deal with you** after your **folly, in that ye have not spoken of me** the thing which is **right, like my servant Job.** Job 42:7-8

One can be rich in faith and poor in material possessions or one can be rich in material possessions and lacking faith (see Jam. 2:5). Job was rich both in faith and in material possessions. Perhaps a cynical question, but I wonder if Job had been a low-income guy who had never experienced the good life, would his obedience and endurance been as firm? Yes, because whatever else, his faith was <u>not</u> exhausted.

Being on the bottom of life is <u>not</u> easy and becomes harder when you try to fight the situation. It takes maturity to accept the condition and then trust God to see you through. It is best to acknowledge the ordeal as part of the process of conformity. It is best to experience the ordeal of suffering as identification with Jesus within you. Suffering may be the only way to know Him and be formed into an obedient son or daughter. Suffering turns off the old man's dynamics and exercises the new man's faith.

Joseph (son of Jacob)

Abraham begat Isaac. Isaac begat Jacob. Jacob had twelve sons. One of the sons, Joseph was sold into slavery by his brothers and sent to Egypt where Potiphar purchased him. Potiphar had a wife that was sexually attractive to Joseph, but

Joseph refused. Why? When Joseph told Potiphar's wife that he could not lay with her, Joseph literally meant that it was not possible (see Gen. 39:9). The presence of the Lord was with Joseph in such a way that Joseph could not access his carnal sinful nature in this act. You can better understand what happened to Joseph if you visualize him as a robot of Jesus, instead of looking for character within Joseph and praise to Joseph. All praise goes to God.

> **And Joseph said unto them, Fear not: for** *am* **I in the place of God?** Gen 50:19

Moses

The Lord is the Prince of Life, the Author of faith and the Overseer of all (see Acts 3:15; Heb. 12:2, 4:13). Natural man is corrupt and deceived by the prince of this world (see Eph. 2:2-3). Meanwhile, God as Author writes the script for His people. Looking at Moses, a case could be made that Moses wrote part of the script. For example, when Moses pleaded with the Lord not to destroy the children of Israel and the Lord repented of the evil, one could state broadly that the actions of man affect the script of the Lord (see Exod. 32:1-14). Not so. Moses is a prophet of God, sent forth more like a robot than a co-author of life. The Lord put His words in Moses' mouth (see Deut. 18:15-18). Moses was obedient in word.

Pharaoh

The Israelites were slaves in Egypt under Pharaoh for over four hundred years (see Gen. 15:13; Exod. 12:41). Afterward, the Lord called Moses to lead the Israelites out of Egypt. Meanwhile, the Lord hardened Pharaoh's heart so that he would not let the Israelites depart until the Lord chose the time (see Exod. 4:21). The Lord delayed the release by Pharaoh and chose to exercise ten plagues in order to show His power (see Exod. 11:9). Was Pharaoh a robot? The Lord controlled

Pharaoh like a robot even though Pharaoh had a human will. The Lord can make things happen to change world events by His ability to control the words and deeds of men during rare periods of intervention.

Gideon

The book of Judges records the history of the children of Israel under a covenant of obedience to blessings. Due to human nature, they were <u>not</u> able to obey and they suffered bondage, which fulfilled the words of Joshua, **"Ye cannot serve the Lord"** (Joshua 24:19). Due to the covenant, the Lord delivered them using judges that were anointed with His Spirit. Gideon was one of these judges.

> **And the angel of the LORD appeared unto him, and said unto him, The LORD** *is* **with thee, thou mighty man of valour.** Jud. 6:12

The Lord delivered the children of Israel from their enemies by empowering Gideon through the Spirit of God. There is no record of Gideon doing anything to merit this favor. He was chosen to do something without any preconditions. The Lord could have given Gideon a revelation to his soul of the deliverance He wanted, but instead chose to lead Gideon along step by step. First, by allowing him to set a fleece as a visual sign and later allowing him to hear of victory from the enemy's camp (see Jud. 6:36-40, 7:15).

Looking at the covenant of obedience to blessings, it may appear easy to obey, but the people did <u>not</u> have the Spirit within them and the powers of evil can be effective against the human nature. The Old Testament covenant had fault (see Heb. 8:7). The fault was the human nature from the corrupt soul inherited from Adam.

Isaiah

Robotics is a contemporary analogy that applies to the prophet Isaiah. When the creation (Isaiah) was in the presence of the Creator, his human heart melted from the majesty and glory. In comparison to the sinful human speech and reasoning, how could Isaiah resist? The thought of saying "no" to God did <u>not</u> exist. The thought of returning and obeying the unclean lips of where he came from did <u>not</u> exist. How could his ability to choose exist in such a glorious environment? "**Here** *am* **I, send me.**" Then he was given a programming task for the people of God (see Isa. 6).

Jeremiah

The prophet Jeremiah wanted to exercise his human will and cease serving God, but the Word overwhelmed him as his human mechanics was consumed and electrified from a heavenly Source.

> **Then I said, I will not make mention of him, nor speak any more in his name. But** *his word* **was in mine heart as a burning fire shut up in my bones, and I was weary with forbearing, and I could not** *stay*. Jer. 20:9

You could speculate that Jeremiah could have resisted based upon I Cor. 14:32, "**And the spirits of the prophets are subject to the prophets**". Yet in context with the church at Corinth, the prophets were admonished to be orderly, decently and without confusion. Jeremiah tried to resist, but was unsuccessful. The Potter has power over the clay.

Ezekiel

To prevent a one directional robot from running into a wall, you must place your hand on the robot and change the direction. The hand of the Lord was strong upon the prophet Ezekiel (see Ezek. 3:14). Furthermore, the Lord made Ezekiel's tongue cleave to the roof of his mouth in order to be silent and opened his mouth when he was to speak (see Ezek. 3:26-27). The free will of Ezekiel did not have a vote in this matter.

Nehemiah

The Babylonians destroyed Jerusalem in 586 BC and carried the Jews into captivity. Later, the Medes and Persians defeated the Babylonians. Afterwards, the Jews started slowly returning to Jerusalem, but many Jews just blended in with the Persians. A Jewish man named Nehemiah rose to the high position of cupbearer for the king of Persia. The king allowed Nehemiah to return to Jerusalem in 446 BC to rebuild the walls.

When the good hand of God is upon you, results will happen to accomplish His will. Nehemiah was riding the wave. On a surfboard, you turn and adjust to stay in the force of the wave because the wave is doing all the work to propel you forward. You could speculate that a surfer could jump off the board or jerk the board against the power of the wave, but wouldn't that be from the control of a destructive nature? A robot of Jesus is plugged into the Source of a gracious God and to resist is against the robot's obedient construction (see Eph. 2:10). Therefore, Nehemiah was successful in rebuilding the walls of Jerusalem (see Neh. 12:27).

Mordecai

In 478 BC, the Persian kingdom ruled the nations. Mordecai was a Jew and the cousin of Esther, queen of Persia. Robotic timing is seen in the lives of Mordecai and others (see Est. 5:14-7:10). Haman, second in command to the king, wanted to annihilate the Jews, starting with Mordecai. Haman was advised by his wife and friends to build gallows to hang

Mordecai on. That same night the king could not sleep and read about Mordecai exposing a plan to lay hands on the king. The next morning the gallows are built and the king hangs Haman on the gallows built for Mordecai. If the gallows were built a day earlier, Mordecai may have been hanged instead. Natural schedules and events may appear unclear to us, but not to God (see Est. 4:14).

Samuel

At times, the Word of God and the intervention of God, relax.

> **And the word of the Lord was precious in those days;** there was **no open vision.**
> I Sam. 3:1b

At rare times, the Lord speaks to man. When the Lord called to young Samuel, he went to Eli the priest. Samuel was young and naive and did not discern the Lord. Also, the Lord wanted Eli to know that He was speaking through Samuel. Later on, notice how the Lord granted results through Samuel, "**And Samuel grew and the Lord was with him, and did let none of his words fall to the ground**" (I Sam. 3:19). The Word of the Lord spoken through Samuel overruled the will of man. Whatever Samuel spoke, the Lord caused to happen.

Beware of evil reports. You can pray that evil reports spoken against you and others, will fall to the ground. Like Satan, evil reports can fall (see Luke 10:18).

King Saul

Saul was Israel's first king. Saul is an example of God allowing the will of the people. "**And Samuel heard all the words of the people, and he rehearsed them in the ears of the Lord. And the Lord said to Samuel, Hearken unto their voice, and make them a king**" (I Sam. 8:21-22). Life and learning is developed through contrasts: seeing what you can do versus seeing what the Lord can do. The Lord told Israel what their chosen king would be like. Then, the Lord put the software into Saul to "make it happen". "**God gave him another heart**" (I Sam. 10:9). This Scripture should weaken the foundation that keeps afloat the stronghold of the pseudo-axiom statement, "*God does not make robots.*" Only the Spirit of God can reveal what happened within Saul's heart. Reason can dilly and dally. Reason assumes that Saul could have been a good king. Reason says that it was Saul's choices that caused his problems. No, it was the people's choice and the Lord gave them a robotic king that did what God put in Saul's heart. Am I over reaching? Perhaps. We do not know what the Lord did with Saul's anointing and later with the evil spirit that troubled Saul. King Saul is complex for he was unable to achieve total obedience to the Lord due to the boundaries established by the Word of the Lord.

King David

David was Israel's second king. David did not interfere with King Saul because David knew the Lord was in control through the anointing upon Saul (See I Sam. 24:6). David rejected his free will to remove Saul as king. Later, when David was anointed, he believed that God could control his words, thoughts and deeds.

> **Set a watch, O LORD, before my mouth; keep the door of my lips. Incline not my heart to *any* evil thing, to practice wicked works with men that work iniquity:** Ps. 141:3-4a

David was called a man after God's heart because he did the will of the Lord (see I Sam. 13:14; Acts 13:22). David sinned when the Lord was not in control (see II Sam. 11). Yet David was a great man because the Lord made him great (see II Sam 7:8-9). Under David, the nation of Israel became great. After David, Israel gradually declined.

Nations

The kings and rulers desire to sever the connection to the command center of the Lord. They want free will. The Lord laughs at how ridiculous that is.

> **The kings of the earth set themselves, and the rulers take counsel together, against the Lord, and against his Anointed,** *saying,* **Let us break their bands asunder, and cast away their cords from us. He that sitteth in the heavens shall laugh: the Lord shall have them in derision.** Ps. 2:2-4

The Lord strengthens one nation and weakens another, because He is Lord (see Ezek. 30:24-26). If a nation went to war and destroyed all enemy nations and the conquering nation was left with only friendly nations, due to the existence of invisible evil forces, some of the friendly nations would become enemies and the conquering nation would be back where it started from before the war (see Obad. 1:7). Due to the depravity of man, the Lord uses one nation to humble another. Later, after the nation He uses becomes prideful, He must judge that nation (see Ezek. 25:6-7).

The word "nation" by association came to mean specifically the Gentiles, the heathen, in contrast to Israel or Judah. God identified Israel as a son, <u>not</u> just a nation (see Hos. 11:1). Israel was to be God's battle-axe to judge the nations, similar to how He destroyed the earth with a flood (see Jer. 51:20). God called Israel to destroy the Gentile nations, which He determined to be sinful beyond repentance (see Deut. 4:38, 6:16). When Israel is addressed as a nation, there is an implication of disobedience to God and backsliding, so that they are like the idolatrous Gentiles (see Deut. 32:28; Jud. 2:20; Isa. 1:4).[1] Often Israel became sinful beyond recognition as a son.

Left alone, the sinful lifestyle of man is not sustainable on earth. Women and children are destroyed (see I Sam. 15:3). If left to prosper, these children would continue to corrupt. When nations worship other gods and violate the holy law, the Lord hears a sour note from His creation. Toleration of this racket is limited. The goal of the Lord is to reveal how life is sustained by repentance to His ways. Yet death is viewed differently between God and man. God can resurrect the dead, while death is final to man.

Israel was not the sole executor of God's judgment. Consider how God announced that the nation of Assyria was the work of His hand, the rod of His anger and the staff in His hand (see Isa. 10:5, 19:25). A rod and a staff are mindless analogies similar to a robot. Scripture highlights detail commands from the Lord to man, such as the sharpening of weapons and the blowing of a trumpet (see Jer. 51:11, 27). Meanwhile, the Lord does not overlook payment for services (see Ezek. 29:18-20). God uses nations for His purpose with the goal to reveal to man that He is Lord. The Lord is in control. Yet He relaxes His hand at times (see Ezek. 20:22). Therefore, nations are part of the overall plan of God. The merger of all people into one world entity was denied at the tower of Babel, but will be allowed in the last days and will be made perfect in the kingdom of God (see Gen 11:9; Rev. 20:8; 21:3, 24-26). Whether national groups, such as Americans are recognized in the kingdom of God is unknown at this time.[2]

Conclusion

Religion starts with God and moves downward to man. Some start with man and imply that man can limit God. God cannot be limited. The principle rings true that God can delve into the affairs of man unabated. Prophetic announcements of the future are fixed due to His ability to do this. However, man is limited in his ability to serve God without the Spirit of God. God is not a Robot to act based upon man's performance, but man is a robot to act for God based upon the Almighty's ability. The will of God does not fluctuate based upon the acts of man. The will of God is stable and the acts of man will be rewarded or judged based upon His standards.

Some believe differently. God is falsely portrayed with a breaking heart due to the failures of man. Scripture disagrees (see Gen. 1:1-Rev. 22:21). God knows the condition of man. The reality is that God cannot be pleased with man without a heart for God and a heart cannot be for God without the Spirit of God. Although man with his conscience can do good in the natural world, Spiritual faith is required to please God in the Spiritual realm (see Heb. 11:6).

The Old Testament is the example (see I Cor. 10:11). The Old Testament sought obedience from the covenant of the law in order to sustain an earthly kingdom (see Lev. 26; Deut. 28). This was to mirror the rule in heaven and the future Kingdom of God. However, the story of the nation of Israel reveals man's inability to accomplish this goal.

Therefore, a new covenant was needed. Israel was expecting another Prophet, the Messiah, so called because of the anointing of the Spirit (see John 4:25). However, their expectations remained fixed on an earthly kingdom, while Jesus came preaching a heavenly kingdom.

Chapter Five

New Testament Robots

The Old Testament was faulty (see Heb. 8:7). The New Testament is better. A higher level of obedience is possible due to a change in man. Holy Spirit is with God's people and His power is able to do God's will, even though the will or soul of man has <u>not</u> changed between covenants. Holy Spirit knows the combination to influence the will of man, just as He did those anointed in the Old Testament.

> **As thou hast given Him power over all flesh,**
> John 17:2a

The following are a few examples of people with human wills that demonstrated obedience in thought, word or deed. They acted like robots of Jesus during rare times.

Disciples

The disciples definitely had a human will and they used it. Yet there were moments when the will of the Lord pacified their will and established a destiny. They followed like sheep or like robots from an electrical current. Jesus was the Word that spoke creation into existence. If you imagine the disciples thinking and choosing when Jesus spoke to them, you do <u>not</u> understand the power of the Word of God over His creation.

The Word does not return void (see Isa. 55:11). When Jesus said, "**Follow me**", they left everything. When Jesus said, "**the sheep of the flock shall be scattered**" they deserted Him (see Matt. 4:19, 26:31). The disciples are examples of robots controlled to follow and then released to scatter. The disciples made mistakes, but the Lord was always there to keep them in line. His will was accomplished through them.

> **God also bearing** *them* **witness, both with signs and wonders, and with divers miracles, and gifts of the Holy Ghost, according to his own will?** Heb. 2:4

A Roman Centurion

Jesus credited a Roman centurion with the greatest faith He had found in Israel.

> **When Jesus heard** *it,* **he marvelled, and said to them that followed, Verily I say unto you, I have not found so great faith, no, not in Israel.** Matt. 8:10

There are three reasons for the great faith of this Roman centurion. First, Jesus wanted to provoke the Jewish people to jealousy and secondly, the Roman government was used by God to establish an environment for the gospel to be heard. A Roman centurion was part of this government (see Rom. 11:14, 13:4). Finally, the centurion heard the Word untainted by Jewish traditions, which brought faith to him (see Rom. 10:17). The Roman centurion is an example of a robot of Jesus outside the awareness of religious people.

Mary (sister of Martha and Lazarus)

> **She hath done what she could: she is come aforehand to anoint my body to the burying.** Mark 14:8

Mary sat at Jesus' feet and heard the Word (see Luke 10:38-42). Days later, Mary poured an expensive perfume on the head of Jesus. I believe Mary was given instructions to anoint Jesus before His burial.

A superficial interpretation would view Mary as deciding to anoint Jesus. The proper interpretation has Mary hearing and obeying.

This is an important distinction. The task to anoint Jesus did <u>not</u> come from Mary. The instruction came from the Lord. Mary was obedient in deed. We should remember Mary as sitting and hearing the Word. This is the memorial to Mary. Martha, her sister, did her own thing by serving instead of hearing. The Lord said that Martha was troubled.

> **And Jesus answered and said unto her, Martha, Martha, thou art careful and troubled about many things: But one thing is needful: and Mary hath chosen that good part, which shall not be taken away from her.** Luke 10:41-42

This is one of the few occurrences in the New Testament where the word "*chosen*" is used in relationship with human decision-making. The majority of the usage of "*chosen*" in the New Testament relates to God. Mary chose to find and do what the Lord wanted, while Martha chose to do what she wanted (free will). Mary is an example of someone who became beautiful to the Lord through obedience.

Paul

Paul was given an important task as an apostle and the Lord made sure it was done right. Paul was made perfect through weakness. Perfection is total obedience or control from a perfect Source. The grace of God operated in Paul when he was made aware of his own inability through the buffeting from a messenger of Satan.

> **And he said unto me, My grace is sufficient for thee: for my strength is made perfect in weakness. Most gladly therefore will I rather glory in my infirmities, that the power of Christ may rest upon me. II Cor. 12:9**

The infirmities of Paul from the messenger of Satan were reproaches, lack of supplies, persecutions and distresses (see II Cor. 12:10). Paul was so weak from the buffeting by the messenger of Satan that he was in a passive state that allowed robotic obedience to the commands of God. Paul is an example of a life controlled by God.

> **But we have this treasure in earthen vessels, that the excellency of the power may be of God, and not of us. II Cor. 4:7**

Peter

Even though Peter had a strong will, he remained a subject of the Spiritual world. Peter acknowledges Jesus as the Son of God by a revelation from the Father in heaven and then rebukes Jesus when Jesus stated His soon coming death in Jerusalem. At one moment Peter is controlled by the Father in heaven and then highly influenced by Satan (see Matt. 16:15-23). Still, Peter recognized the ability of the Lord to control, even to the level of walking on water (see Matt. 14:28). How did this happen? Peter watched and understood the power that

Jesus had over men and the earthly elements. Peter asked the Lord to issue a command for him to come toward Jesus. A robot that is given a command to move forward can illustrate this. This is a small microcosm of the Christian life. Robotics is rare. Faith comes to do a miracle, such as a new heart (salvation) or a healing, etc. and then we are responsible to continue on. Peter saw the winds and sank. Yet Peter called out again to the Control Center (Jesus) and was rescued.

Still, the robot analogy is lacking. The creation of man by God is greater than a creation of a robot by man, since the complex will of man can call out to the Creator while a man-made robot can only act.

Had free will prevailed, Peter would have remained a commercial fisherman hidden under the covers of history. Instead, Jesus was the Author and Finisher of Peter's faith (see Heb. 12:2). The Lord even authored Peter's manner of death. Peter had no choice. Peter is someone with a strong human will, who was unable to do his own thing.

> **Verily, verily, I say unto thee, When thou wast young, thou girdest thyself, and walkedst whither thou wouldest: but when thou shalt be old, thou shalt stretch forth thy hands, and another shall gird thee, and carry** *thee* **whither thou wouldest not. This spake he, signifying by what death he should glorify God. And when he had spoken this, he saith unto him, Follow me.** John 21:18-19

The Church at Philippi

Has the Lord given the church free will so that He will not interfere with his or her right to choose? Some say, "Yes, that you choose to obey," but that is a mental activity. Instead, the New Testament church has the power of God working in them. The church is called to be holy or separated from self-will, the world and the devil. The church is called to be perfect by complete obedience to the will of God.

> **Wherefore, my beloved, as ye have always obeyed, not as in my presence only, but now much more in my absence, work out your own salvation with fear and trembling. For it is God which worketh in you both to will and to do of** *his* **good pleasure.** Phil. 2:12-13

Did the church at Philippi obey all the time? No. Rightly divided, this means they excelled in obedience. The fear and trembling was due to the weakness that was necessary before the Lord took control. I speculate there were times, perhaps just seconds, when they acted like robots, as Jesus worked in them.

The Scripture above does not imply that works must complete salvation. Salvation is by grace through faith. The free gift of faith is active DNA from God that will produce good works. Salvation without faith does not exist, nor does faith exist without works (see Jam. 2:17).

Notice the order within the Scripture above. God is the Initiator. He does two things here (**both to will and to do**). He influenced their will and He directed their actions for His good pleasure. This is the same order of salvation — you will call upon the Name of the Lord after He has changed your nature (see Rom. 10:13).

The Church at Ephesus

I cannot find Scripture where God left the church out of His realm of influence. I do find Scripture where the church can be ignorant of the influence of Christ (see Rev. 3:17).

> **Now unto him that is able to do exceeding abundantly above all that we ask or think,**

> **according to the power that worketh in us,** Eph. 3:20

Paul writes that the Lord is able to operate through the Ephesian church and do things they were unaware of: things that were above their realm of thought and supplication. This appears to be the blindness today with the "*God does not make robots*" philosophy. Still, the Lord has the ability through the power within His church to operate in total obedience and many are unaware of it. Have you ever said something and wondered, "Why *did I say that?*" Have you ever done something and asked, "*Why did I do that?*" Have you ever thought something and asked, "*Where did that thought come from?*" Has someone every said or done something that caused you to ponder, "*Where did that come from?*" If so, you may understand the robot analogy. Still, we are responsible for the words and deeds from our soul when the Spiritual forces are not in control.

The Church at Colossae

The robot analogy is about a thought, word or deed controlled by Holy Spirit without any influence from the human will in order for His church to be filled, to walk, to work, to increase, to be powerful, patient, longsuffering and joyful.

> **That ye might be filled with the knowledge of his will in all wisdom and spiritual understanding; That ye might walk worthy of the Lord unto all pleasing, being fruitful in every good work, and increasing in the knowledge of God; Strengthened with all might, according to his glorious power, unto all patience and longsuffering with joyfulness;** Col. 1:9b-11

"**Walking worthy of the Lord unto all pleasing**" is a high bar that the human nature cannot reach. This is the faith of God in action within the Spiritual nature of these believers. This is Paul's prayer for them. This is not beyond the realm of possibility. This does stifle free will. The robot analogy fits here with all the operations of His will, wisdom and ability. The struggle is when pride can raise its head during occurrences at this level. Perhaps a hint to why these occurrences are rare, lest the believer boast.

Conclusion

The purpose of creation and the theme of Scripture is unity with a glorious God and Savior. In order to be in God's family you must act like God (see Luke 8:21). Anyone who sins must die. All have sinned. Jesus came and died in our place, which satisfied the payment for not obeying the commandments. Then God changes hearts and imparts Holy Spirit and faith in order to obey the commandments. We suffer as our flesh is being put to death and we have joy as Holy Spirit comforts. Meanwhile, the Word of God is renewing our minds, as we understand what our calling is. Renewing the mind is a major part. This is the progressive growth of Christians to become obedient to a high level similar to a robot, in that we do His will exclusively. Meanwhile, free will philosophy hinders.

This chapter contains selective readings from the New Testament that demonstrate the robot analogy. There are other New Testament Scriptures where the analogy can be found.

Chapter Six

Robots in Reverse

When Jesus walked on the earth, the scribes, Pharisees, Sadducees and Sanhedrin were the arbiters of theology, doctrine and the governing rules within Judaism. Today, denominational leaders establish doctrine. Sometimes, they can miss it. Why? Carnal thoughts are not the same as Spiritual. The common mistake is to establish an earthly rule. The Jewish leaders of Israel desired an earthly rule. This mistake is common from reasoning. Reasoning can disagree with the Word of God. A conflict exists between Scripture and human reasoning. Even God's people try to direct control from earth, instead of heaven. Control is the main issue in this disagreement. Again and again, God exhorts men that there is a problem with your thinking.

> **Trust in the LORD with all thine heart; and lean not unto thine own understanding. In all thy ways acknowledge him, and he shall direct thy paths.** Prov. 3:5-6

This conflict can be in complete disagreement. Man can rely upon his own understanding. Reasoning can turn from Scripture and slide. Man can reverse from trust in the Lord to reasoning. Like a robot cannot change its hard wiring, sometimes Christians, cannot change his or her harden belief without the Creator's intervention. God exhorts man to renew his carnal mind, to transform his mind by the Word (see Rom. 12:2; II Tim. 3:16). Carnal doctrine equates to carnal thinking that cannot please God (see Rom. 8:6-8). Consider the Corinthian church. Some in the church focused on man for their Spiritual change (see I Cor. 1:12a). Likewise, the Galatian church reasoned that the law was necessary to complete their sojourn (see Gal. 3:1-5). Even the apostle Peter reasoned that he should not eat with the Gentiles (see Gal. 2:11-14).

The Word is Spiritual. To be Spiritual minded, a proper interpretation of what the Bible breathes is necessary for perfection and good works (see II Tim. 3:15-17). The following are some common examples of flipping the meaning and running the robot in reverse. Nevertheless, human reasoning cannot reverse what God does (see Isa. 43:13).

The Apostle Paul

Some believe the apostle Paul was the greatest Christian that ever lived. Who Paul was, was due to what the Lord did to Paul. However, Paul is falsely credited for *"getting the numbers up"* (see I Cor. 3:6). One pastor led his congregation to give a round of applause to the great apostle Paul.[1] This is human reasoning and a reversal of Scripture. Paul described himself as the chief sinner, the least saint and the least apostle.

> **This *is* a faithful saying, and worthy of all acceptation that Christ Jesus came into the world to save sinners; of whom I am chief.** I Tim. 1:15

> **Unto me, who am less than the least of all saints, is this grace given, that I should preach among the Gentiles the unsearchable riches of Christ:** Eph. 3:8

> **For I am the least of the apostles, that am not meet to be called an apostle, because I persecuted the church of God.** I Cor. 15:9

Paul is an example of the grace of God. Left to self, Paul was fierce in his persecution of Christians (see Acts 9:1). If free will had prevailed, Paul would have been a great deterrent to Christianity. After conversion, Paul needed a thorn in his flesh to keep him from exalting himself (see II Cor. 12:7). Paul demonstrates the Spirit of Jesus controlling a chief sinner to do commands to build and edify His church. Paul was like a robot of Jesus and confessed that he was <u>not</u> doing it (see underline of Scripture below).

> **But by the grace of God I am what I am: and his grace which** *was bestowed* **upon me was not in vain; but I laboured more abundantly than they all:** <u>*yet* **not** I</u>**, but the grace of God which was with me.** I Cor. 15:10

Paul is admired for what he did for us. This is human reasoning. As one minister put it, '*When I get to heaven, I'm going to find brother Paul, I'm going to get hold of that boy. I'm going to hug him and I'm going to say, "Paul, Chapter 7 of Romans saved my life."*'[2] However, it was really the grace of God working through Paul. The control was from heaven.

The Thief on the Cross

Human reasoning has reversed the thief on the cross. Some say he got in by the skin of his teeth or he avoided hell by a small margin.

> **And one of the malefactors which were hanged railed on him, saying, If thou be Christ, save thyself and us. But the other answering rebuked him, saying, Dost not**

> **thou fear God, seeing thou art in the same condemnation? And we indeed justly; for we receive the due reward of our deeds: but this man hath done nothing amiss. And he said unto Jesus, Lord, remember me when thou comest into thy kingdom. And Jesus said unto him, Verily I say unto thee, Today shalt thou be with me in paradise.** Luke 23:39-43

Timing is 95% of the will of God. The cross of Christ was prime time in the history of the world. We need to go back a few hours before the crucifixion to appreciate the magnitude of the thief's words. A dramatic change occurred at the Mount of Olives. The powers of darkness started having their time. Jesus started experiencing physical suffering during His arrest and trial. He was experiencing emotional suffering with the abandonment of His disciples and the accusations from the Jewish leaders. These sufferings escalate to the cross several hours later.

Yet with the thief beside Him another change occurs. Someone believes in Him again. It appears that the words of the thief encouraged Jesus. What a feat; to encourage the Son of God at His most vulnerable hour. At His crucifixion, the Father reserved a special position beside Jesus for this thief (see Luke 23:33). In the future kingdom, the Father may grant this thief the seat on the right side of Jesus. This is the position coveted by the sons of thunder (see Mark 10:37). Jesus asked the sons of thunder if they were able to drink of the cup that He was to drink of. The thief was crucified in the same manner as Jesus, although the thief did _not_ experience the same cup. Has the Father reserved the same position in His kingdom? Consider how Holy Spirit spoke through the apostles about Jesus returning like a thief in the night.

- Apostle Paul:

  For yourselves know perfectly that the day of the Lord so cometh as a <u>thief</u> in the night. 1 Thes. 5:2

- Apostle Peter:

  But the day of the Lord will come as a <u>thief</u> in the night; II Pet. 3:10a

- Apostle John:

  Behold I come as a <u>thief</u> in the night: Rev. 16:15a

The thief on the cross did little for us and we do <u>not</u> honor a thief. In heaven, it might be reversed. The Father may honor the thief by placing him on the right side of Jesus. This position might bring the Father pleasure (see Eph. 1:5).

Salvation

There are two separate salvations in Scripture that require a scrupulous division of the Word (see II Tim. 2:15). These are often blended together, but they are separate and unique. The Jews were looking for a national salvation (see Acts 1:6). Jesus came preaching a Spiritual salvation. Every man will either perish or inherit eternal life, but sins can be forgiven in the natural salvation of a nation or the Spiritual salvation in the Kingdom of heaven (see Lev. 4:20-35; I John 2:12). The Old Testament salvation with payment from bulls and goats, and forgiveness of sins, was a shadow of the New Testament with the Blood of Jesus and regeneration of the heart of man.

1) National or Natural Salvation (see Deut. 28; Isa. 1:19)
   - Repentance is necessary

- Obedience to law
- Conscience of right and wrong, no Spiritual discernment
- Sustains earthly culture
- Earthly or Natural kingdom
- Exalts a nation
- Old Testament
- Continues in New Testament times (see Rom. 2:14)

2) Spiritual Salvation or Regeneration (see II Cor. 5:17)
   - Contingent on election or God's will
   - Kingdom of heaven
   - Imparted faith
   - Repentance is evidence of
   - Holy Spirit sealed in heart
   - Jesus as Savior, Author and High Priest
   - Old Testament and New Testament saints (see Heb. 11)

Christians have a new nature and should realize the unsaved do <u>not</u> have this new nature (see I Thes. 4:12). After salvation, the Spirit craves for the believer to exercise faith by doing good works. This can cloud a false sense of the salvation experience and lead the Christian's carnal mind into thinking that it takes an effort on man's part for salvation to occur. Additionally, Christians observe the laws and commands of the Old Testament and forget that these apply to a natural salvation of an earthly kingdom. Meanwhile, Christians forget the hopeless condition they were in prior to salvation and create doctrines of cooperation with God implying, *"You must do your part."*

Spiritual salvation is impossible by man's efforts. Man cannot humble himself, pray, raise his hand high enough, walk an aisle, turn toward God or do any act, law or commandment that will save him. Spiritual Salvation is an act of God alone. Reasoning can reverse it and assume that any small act by man opens the door for God to act and salvation to occur.

God does <u>not</u> perform Spiritual regeneration in response to the natural activity of man. However, the natural culture can be sustained based upon the natural activity of repentance.

Obedience

Human reasoning can seduce the Christian into believing that a high level of obedience is unattainable. The expectation of obedience for the unsaved should be at the bottom while at the top for the Christian. It appears that more obedience is expected from the unsaved to be saved and once saved, a lower standard of obedience is expected of the Christian. This is a reversal. I hear Christians say, "*I sin everyday*", "*I fail miserably*" or "*obviously, we are going to fail.*" Christianity is <u>not</u> just a passive state of confessing failure. Lead by Holy Spirit, the Christian has the capacity to act like a robot of Jesus. <u>Not</u> legalism and <u>not</u> unable to sin, but evidence of a child of God.

> **And God *is* able to make all grace abound toward you; that ye, always having all sufficiency in all *things*, may abound to <u>every good work</u>:** II Cor. 9:8

There is a fight of faith and a wrestling with forces, but Holy Spirit enables a high level of obedience. The Christian mind should be renewed to this possibility. Jesus said, "**be perfect**" while reasoning says, "You can never be perfect." (cf. Matt. 5:48)

Impossible

Salvation is personal. Each one should examine his or her heart to determine if they are in the faith (see II Cor. 13:5). Free will Christians who believe that someone can renounce their salvation, believe this applied toward others, while boasting that they themselves will most definitely remain in the faith.[3] They recognize their works such as church attendance and moral acts as keeping them in the faith, although they do not admit salvation by works (see Phil. 2:12). This is similar to the boastful attitude of Peter to remain with Jesus, while assuming that others would depart (see Mark 14:29).

The classical interpretation of Hebrews 6:4-6 is that you can be saved and fall away or renounce your salvation. The word "**impossible**" is reversed. Some cannot accept that it is impossible to renounce your salvation, so they reverse it to possible.

> **4 For *it is* impossible for those who were once enlightened, and have tasted of the heavenly gift, and were made partakers of the Holy Ghost, 5 And have tasted the good word of God, and the powers of the world to come, 6 *If* they shall fall away, to renew them again unto repentance; seeing they crucify to themselves the Son of God afresh, and put *him* to an open shame.** Heb. 6:4-6

I challenge the translation of the conditional conjunction "*if*" at Heb. 6:6 in the King James Version. This challenge is easily won based upon the Greek text. "*If*" was inserted to make good English, but it reverses the context of something impossible to something possible. "*If*" reverses the statement to a conditional statement. The word "*and*" is the actual translation, not "*if*". The New International Version (NIV) correctly uses the word "*and*", not "*if*". Below is a "word for word" presentation from The New Greek-English Interlinear New Testament. (see underline of "**and**")

> **For [it is] impossible for the ones once having been enlightened, both having tasted of the gift heavenly and having become partners of [the] Holy Spirit and having tasted [the] good Word of God and [the] powers of the coming age <u>and</u> having fallen away, to renew again**

to repentance, crucifying to themselves the Son of God and holding [Him] up to contempt.[4]

(In the Scripture above, single brackets [ ] indicate the enclosed word(s) in the text is disputed. Some have criticized me for <u>not</u> placing the article "the" in front of Holy Spirit. In the Scripture above, the article is absent because the Person is meant, <u>not</u> the personality. You would <u>not</u> write that you have become partners with "the" John Doe.)

Below is the actual Greek: One of the most beautiful things that human eyes can behold. Please, focus on the words that I have underlined for simplicity.

4 <u>Ἀδύνατον</u> γὰρ τοὺς ἅπαξ φωτισθέντας γευσαμένους τε τῆς δωρεᾶς τῆς ἐπουρανίου <u>καὶ</u> μετόχους γενηθέντας πνεύματος ἁγίου

5 <u>καὶ</u> καλὸν γευσαμένους θεοῦ ῥῆμα δυνάμεις τε μέλλοντος αἰῶνος,

6 <u>καὶ</u> παραπεσόντας, πάλιν ἀνακαινίζειν εἰς μετάνοιαν, ἀνασταυροῦντας ἑαυτοῖς τὸν υἱὸν τοῦ θεοῦ <u>καὶ</u> παραδειγματίζοντας.

The first word underlined is the Greek word "adynaton" which is translated "**impossible**". It means:

- Powerless,
- Could <u>not</u> do,
- Impotent,
- <u>Not</u> possible,
- and weak.

The next words underlined are four occurrences of "kai" which are translated "**and**". "Kai" is translated as the English function word "**and**" over eight thousand times in the New Testament. There are only four occurrences of "kai" in this text, but six translated English words (five translated "**and**" and one translated "*if*"). In other words, there is less Greek and more English. This verse is the only place in the King James Version of the New Testament where "kai" is translated "*if*".

Five descriptions of Spiritual salvation are noted. 1) They are enlightened, 2) have Spiritually tasted of the heavenly gift, 3) made partners of Holy Ghost, 4) tasted the good Word of God and 5) the powers of the world to come. The writer is describing a salvation act of regeneration through faith. After you read the five descriptions of salvation and come upon the "*if,*" you forget the "**impossible**" context of the verse, since "*if*" implies a condition that is possible. A correct context can be illustrated by a simple paraphrase where the five descriptions of salvation are summed into one.

> It is impossible to be saved and having fallen away.

It is impossible (powerless) for man to save himself and it is impossible (powerless) for those saved to fall away (see Matt. 10:27). Jesus has all power in the Spiritual realm. Jesus would have to release you from His hand in order to fall away (see John 10:28). Since man has limited ability in the natural realm, he often assumes ability in the Spiritual.

> **And Jesus came and spake unto them, saying, All power is given unto me in heaven and in earth.** Matt. 28:18

There is a difference between an actual occurrence of an event and a doctrinal statement for edification. Hebrews 6:4-6 is not an actual occurrence of falling away, but a doctrinal statement in order to move forward into maturity. An actual occurrence would exist within a historical context, such as in the book of Acts. I cannot find an actual occurrence of salvation such as Lydia (see Acts 16:14) "**whose heart the Lord opened**" and then an actual occurrence of falling away such as "Lydia fell away after the Lord opened her heart" (not in Scripture). Some refer to Demas whom departed from Paul, but just because you are around Paul does not prove salvation occurred (see II Tim. 4:10).

Meanwhile, Hebrews 6:4-6 with the conditional "*if*" is used as a point of reference to revisit and add meaning to other Scripture.

> **And I give unto them eternal life; and they shall never perish, neither shall any** *man* **pluck them out of my hand. My Father, which gave** *them* **me, is greater than all; and no** *man* **is able to pluck** *them* **out of my Father's hand.**
> John 10:28-29

The classic added assumption in the Scripture above is that you can pluck yourself out of Jesus' hand based upon the classic interpretation of Hebrews 6:4-6. This is a reversal.

Some translations, such as the American Standard Version, link the word "**impossible**" with repentance. Those saved and then fall away— it is impossible to renew them again to repentance. However, the Greek language places important words or phrases at the beginning for emphasis, and this would rearrange the context. The context emphasizes the impossibility of falling away.

Hebrews 6:4-6 is a hypothetic hyperbole. The writer of Hebrews knows that falling away (hypothetic, not an actual occurrence) would require extreme measures (hyperbole), such as Jesus being crucified again in order to keep His elect in His hand. These are impossible events. It is impossible to renew again to repentance. It is impossible to crucify to themselves the Son of God afresh. It is impossible to put Him to an open shame again. A robot of Jesus is Spiritually minded and does not think disobediently. It is a disobedient thought to assume that you can renounce your salvation and override the power of God toward salvation.

- Disobedient Doubt=I can backslide and renounce my gift of salvation.
- Obedient Faith=No one can separate me from My Savior, including myself.

Finally, a case could be made that it is a violation of the third commandment to believe that you can renounce salvation. Someone has called upon the name of the Lord, was saved, and the name of the Lord was in vain because the salvation was not completed (see Exod. 20:7; Rom. 10:13). The writer of Hebrews was trying to eliminate these vain thoughts and move the believer toward perfection (see Heb. 6:1,19).

The Great Commission

The Great Commission is a call to discipleship. Some reverse it to evangelism only (see Mark 16:15). The commission is 1) evangelism, 2) baptism and 3) discipleship. You could also include 4) signs (see Mark 16:17-18).

> **And Jesus came and spake unto them, saying, All power is given unto me in heaven and in earth. Go ye therefore, and teach all nations, baptizing them in the name of the Father, and of the Son, and of the Holy Ghost: Teaching them to observe all things whatsoever I have commanded you: and, lo, I am with you always,** *even* **unto the end of the world. Amen.** Matt. 28:18-20

What does the above text state? First, Jesus has all power and He is with us. Next, go and preach and teach all nations.

Baptize them. Teach them to be obedient through discipleship. They are to learn to obey commands from Jesus.

Conversion happens by His Spirit usually through preaching (see Rom. 10:14) but <u>not</u> always (see Acts 9:5). Like the wind, we do <u>not</u> control where it goes, but we see the results. We go and teach His results (converts) to do everything He has commanded, <u>not</u> neglecting baptism. Still, the Spirit of Jesus controls salvation. Jesus can regenerate a Muslim's heart in the middle of the night in the middle of a Muslim country or He can regenerate a twelve-year-olds heart while hearing his father preach from the pulpit. Jesus controls conversions. Only God can make a Spiritual decision. We are responsible for the discipleship.

This does <u>not</u> imply that we just sit around and let Jesus save. However, can you lead someone to the Lord? Only the Father can lead someone to His Son (see John 6:44, 65, 70). Can you lead a blind man to Jesus and ask the blind man to make Jesus the Healer of his eyes? No. Can you persuade the blind man to accept and let Jesus heal his eyes? No. Jesus may heal his eyes, but the choice comes from Jesus. Observe the below Scripture (see underline).

> **And other fell on <u>good</u> ground, and sprang up, and bare fruit a hundredfold. And when he had said these things, he cried, He that hath ears to hear, let him hear.** Luke 8:8

A key word "**good**" in the parable of the sower is the same Greek word "agathos" that Jesus used to refer to the nature of God.

> **And Jesus said unto him, Why callest thou me <u>good</u>? none is <u>good</u>, save one,** *that is,* **God.** Luke 18:19

In the parable of the sower, before the Word hit the soil, the nature of the soil was changed to "**good**," the same nature as Jesus. Therefore, the new birth occurs independent of any human work or human will.

> **Which were born, not of blood, nor of the will of the flesh, nor of the will of man, but of God.** John 1:13

The Lord changes the nature of the soil before the seed hits the soil. Likewise, the Lord changes a heart before or during the preaching of the Word. The Lord controls the Spiritual realm.

Here are some of the examples of reversing the meaning to evangelism.

The Local Church:

I have often heard that the reason my church is <u>not</u> filled is because the people have <u>not</u> done enough to reach others. This is based on human reasoning. Everyone should do his or her part, but even when the Lord adds to the church, the focus is often on human efforts. Who gets the glory? Who has the power? God may use a human vessel, but no human credit should be given from the pulpit, newsletter or conversation.

> **Who then is Paul, and who *is* Apollos, but ministers by whom ye believed, even as the Lord gave to every man? I have planted, Apollos watered; but God gave the increase. So then neither is he that planteth any thing, neither he that watereth; but God that giveth the increase.** I Cor. 3:5-7

In order to strengthen a message for Christians to witness, the preacher should be an example with results. Messages are often loaded with Scripture and the ratio of Christians to non-Christians and the consequences for the unsaved, but practical application is often absent. I would like to hear how the preacher does it; an example of visiting the market and sharing the gospel with results would be practical.

Pastors use human reasoning. I speak the truth in love in order to demonstrate how reasoning can reverse the great commission away from discipleship — toward money to build a large building, instead of discipling the sheep the Lord has chosen. Do preachers believe that they cannot witness without people believing they are only after their money? One pastor said that I was in a better position to reach a mutual friend, implying that the unsaved view financial gain as the motive of preachers. From my observation, two pastors were reluctant to financially support a widow that had no family (see I Tim. 5:16). An accountant told me that preachers never report to the IRS, additional revenue from revival meetings. Three different Southern Baptist preachers stated they would knowingly take lottery-winnings given into their ministry and plead the Blood of Jesus over this sin. These are a few suspicious things I've observed in my limited circle. There is nothing wrong with a large church, yet I wonder; has a large congregation and a beautiful structure replaced the Jewish circumcision as the new sign of the gospel? I hope not.

The Faithful Members

Meanwhile, church members are encouraged to perform, which is fine and many do. I have constructed a vision of the ideal church member given over time. The ideal member would attend all services, tithe and give offerings, serve in teaching, sing, visit, distribute food/clothing, do ground maintenance, with a national or international mission trip to round out the vision. Again, this is fine. The problem happens when other members believe they do not measure up when they observe the recognition that these ideal members receive. They may feel incomplete (see Gal. 5:26). However, they may be doing exactly what the Lord has prepared for them. Meanwhile, you do not want to discourage those who are going on mission trips and other activities. I do not have a solution for this, but I believe a solution exists. Meanwhile, Jesus thought the ideal church member was a blind beggar that He could heal for the glory of God (see John 9:1-11).

> **And ye are complete in him, which is the head of all principality and power:** Col. 2:10

Meanwhile, Jesus recognized money, but not as we might think.

> **And Jesus sat over against the treasury, and beheld how the people cast money into the treasury: and many that were rich cast in much. And there came a certain poor widow, and she threw in two mites, which make a farthing. And he called** *unto him* **his disciples, and saith unto them, Verily I say unto you, That this poor widow hath cast more in, than all they which have cast into the treasury: For all** *they* **did cast in of their abundance; but she of her want did cast in all that she had,** *even* **all her living.** Mark 12:41-44

Jesus rebuked works, but not as the Pharisees thought.

> **Woe unto you, scribes and Pharisees, hypocrites! for ye compass sea and land to make one proselyte,** Matt. 23:15a

If we have done what the Lord has told us to do, why should we need recognition? Jesus says "no" to recognition:

> **So likewise ye, when ye shall have done all those things which are commanded you, say, We are unprofitable servants: we have done that which was our duty to do.** Luke 17:10

10/40 Window:

The 10/40 Window is an area of the world that contains the largest population of non-Christians in the world. The area extends from 10 degrees to 40 degrees North of the equator and stretches from North Africa across to China. Those who are evangelizing this area are doing the command to go into the entire world. I have heard of this area for many years and know that it is a matter of concern. I appreciate those who have made it a matter of prayer and outreach. There is a difference between trying to "get the numbers up" and Jesus sending out workers into His harvest. This area illustrates that Jesus controls evangelism. This is a modern day example, similar to the disciples going fishing and <u>not</u> catching anything (see John 21:3). The will of Christians, including myself is that this area contain a large Christian population. This is similar to the wealth of this world; an equal distribution is the desire, but Jesus said the poor would always be among us. It is also unfair for the unrighteous to rejoice and the righteous to suffer. All will be sorted out at the day of the Lord. Those who want to "get the numbers up" are being presumptuous. Bad things happen when the people of God presumptuously enter the enemies' camp (see Num. 14:40-45). At times, the apostle Paul wisely withdrew and fled the enemies' camp (see Acts 9:24-25, 19:9). You should <u>not</u> test the Lord thy God (see Matt. 4:7).

Through reasoning, man sends. Through prayer, the Lord sends. One ministry, the Window International Network, prays first for the unreached in the 10/40 window. Ultimately, Jesus controls evangelism with His power to call servants into His harvest. The Great Commission should be titled the Work of Discipleship. Once saved, the work of the Great Commission is primarily discipleship in order for His elect to know His will and do it. Consider that Jesus told Peter to **"Feed My sheep"**, which is discipleship (see John 21:16).

Perish

The most obvious reversal is the word "**perish**" to mean everlasting conscience torment in hell. This is the eternal retribution doctrine based upon selective Scriptures and human reasoning. Advocates reason that this is irresistible bait to catch or persuade a ton of sinners. The duration in hell is intensified. This comes from a belief that salvation is a mental choice or a choice of the human will. The reasoning does make sense. Why spend eternity in hell? Nevertheless, this is hardball religion. There is a hell and a lake of fire with awful suffering, but the duration is ended after the judgment and wrath of God is satisfied (see Rom. 9:28; II Thes. 1:8-9). God is merciful and His anger is temporary (see Ps. 103:8-9). His wrath will torment, but not continually. Once justice has been met, the torment will cease.

The eternal retribution doctrine has been touted to encourage evangelism. From my experience, it does the opposite; it stifles and mortifies. As a new convert to Christianity, the eternal retribution doctrine would trouble me. My emotional soul has been damaged from preaching and teaching that produced anxious thoughts. I sought comfort, but the material I read only defended the doctrine. It did not explain the justice of the doctrine from Scripture. For example, the advocates taught that perish does not mean annihilation. They would go off course, with presumptuous rhetoric such as *"clear teaching," "plainly stated,"* and *"from the lips of Jesus,"* but they could not back it up with Scripture. The eternal retribution doctrine has more support from Christian writings than from Scripture. The doctrine is more of a manmade judgment concerning the unsaved than a judgment from God toward the unsaved. I became suspicious. Do these people know what they are talking about or are they just trying to intimidate and manipulate? I am also suspicious of those who testify that they went to and returned from hell and they heard popular catchphrases in hell, such as *"The Lord told me that I am here because I did not accept Him and give Him my heart,"* instead of phrases in line with Scripture. The following are Scriptures the eternal retribution advocates use:

> **And these shall go away into everlasting punishment: but the righteous into life eternal.** Matt. 25:46

A private and simplistic interpretation states that since the righteous continually exist, the unrighteous do also. However, all Scripture should define a doctrine. Everlasting punishment is further defined in Scripture with the unsaved perishing and consumed in the fire, while eternal life is further defined by the righteous eating from the fruit of the tree of life and permanently existing like God (see John 3:16; I John 3:2; Rev. 22:14).

> **And the devil that deceived them was cast into the lake of fire and brimstone, where the beast and the false prophet** *are*, **and shall be tormented <u>day and night</u> for ever and ever.** Rev. 20:10

"For ever and ever" in the Scripture above literally means "into the ages of the ages". The inclusion of "**day and night**" in Revelation 20:10 merits the meaning to fall in line with other Scripture. "**Day and night**" is cemented on this text. This should be included in the interpretation. There was a first day of creation and there will be a last day of judgment. Day and night will cease. These are <u>not</u> endless.

> **And whosoever was not found written in the book of life was cast into the lake of fire.** Rev. 20:15

> **For God so loved the world, that he gave his only begotten Son, that whosoever believeth in him should not perish, but have everlasting life.** John 3:16

Perish means annihilation. Otherwise, the lake of fire has daytime and nighttime and will contain a larger number of individuals than heaven. The parable of the rich man and Lazarus is presumptuously used to imply never-ending conscious torment in hell (see Luke 16:19-31). I do not challenge the conscious torment, but a closer look at this Scripture implies a limited period of torment due to the limited period of the rich man's earthly life of self-indulgence and apathy toward Lazarus. There is no reference in this parable to a never-ending state in hell. Therefore, I challenge the belief in the immortality of every soul. When God breathed into man the breath of life, man became a living soul, not an immortal soul (see Gen. 2:7). When man ate of the tree of good and evil, he became aware of good and evil. He did not become like God to live forever. To live forever required eating of the tree of life, which the Lord prevented in the garden.

> **And the LORD God said, Behold, the man is become as one of us, to know good and evil: and now, lest he put forth his hand, and take also of the tree of life, and eat, and live for ever: Therefore the LORD God sent him forth from the garden of Eden, to till the ground from whence he was taken. So he drove out the man; and he placed at the east of the garden of Eden Cherubims, and a flaming sword which turned every way, to keep the way of the tree of life.** Gen. 3:22-24

The mortal soul does not live forever. The Lord kept the man away from the tree of life in order to prevent this (see Gen. 3:22). Only God has immortality.

> **Which in his times he shall shew,** *who is* **the blessed and only Potentate, the King of kings, and Lord of lords; Who only hath immortality, dwelling in the light which no**

> **man can approach unto; whom no man hath seen, nor can see: to whom** *be* **honour and power everlasting. Amen** I Tim. 6:15-16

The Greek philosopher Plato (428-348 BC) taught the immortality of the soul. Many Christians liked it and included it in their end time doctrine. Suspiciously, the Westminster Confession of Faith (Chapter IV, 2) references Luke 23:43 as support for the immortal soul.

> **And Jesus said unto him, Verily I say unto thee, Today shalt thou be with me in paradise.** Luke 23:43

I do not understand how they can interpret an immortal soul from Luke 23:43 above. The confession also references Gen. 2:7, Eccl. 12:7 and Matt. 10:28.[5] His mercy endures forever, not His wrath (see Num. 25:11). They will suffer destruction in hell and be annihilated (see Ps. 104:35). Consider the below Scripture which states that God is able to destroy those in hell.

> **And fear not them which kill the body, but are not able to kill the soul: but rather fear him which is able to destroy both soul and body in hell.** Matt. 10:28

The apostle Paul taught that this mortality must put on immortality. The mortal or perishable vessel is changed for the Christian, so they will not perish.

> **In a moment, in the twinkling of an eye, at the last trump: for the trumpet shall sound, and the dead shall be raised incorruptible, and we shall be changed. For this corruptible** *must* **put on incorruption, and this mortal must put on immortality.** I Cor. 15:52-53

The most hated doctrine for me is the doctrine of eternal retribution. Some Christians like it. They believe this doctrine is like throwing a bucket of hot water on a sleepy sinner in order to awaken them to reality. They want to create an offer that man cannot refuse, but in reality they create an offer that man cannot understand. God implants faith, but man tries to implant fear to manipulate. Eternal retribution is a mental accent salvation attempt based upon the belief that the free will of man initiates salvation (see Rom. 10:13).

Where their worm dieth not, and the fire is not quenched. Mark 9:44, 46, 48

Someone quoted Mark 9:44 (above) to support the eternal retribution doctrine. I asked what the word "**worm**" meant? They said the unsaved. I disagreed. The other occurrence of the word "**worm**" in the New Testament is Acts 12:23 where King Herod was "**eaten of worms.**" The word "**worm**" could be inferred to Satan, being the prince of the unsaved. However, I do not believe there is undisputable evidence in this Scripture to reverse the meaning of solid words such as "**perish**", "**destruction**" and "**the fire that consumes**" (see Deut. 9:3). The unsaved will be judged according to his or her conscious words and deeds, cast into the lake of fire and consumed or annihilated (see Heb. 12:29). However, the fire may endure continually or be permanent. Others believe a permanent fire will sustain life, love and light for the righteous.[6]

Perish should be interpreted in context. Perish can mean death of a culture from ungodly lifestyles in a natural context and perish can mean annihilation in the lake of fire within an end-time context. Repentance will sustain a culture from perishing in a natural context, but Spiritual regeneration is required for a permanent existence.

There is a hell and a lake of fire. These are terrible places. The unsaved will be cast there. There will be conscious suffering. However, if the duration were permanent, it would be merciful not to consider parenthood to avoid this permanent afterlife. However, the duration will be limited until the judgment and wrath of God has been satisfied. They will perish. My conscience will <u>not</u> allow me to change the word "**perish**" to mean eternal. A robot of Jesus is hard wired by the Word and free of hardball religion (the fruit of human reasoning).

Eternal

Why do those who establish doctrines change the meaning of "**perish**" to "**eternal**"? Because they see the words, "**eternal**," "**everlasting**," and "**forever and ever**" in the translated text. Secondly, there is <u>not</u> enough support in the denominational leadership. People are apathetical. However, in these times of information, the Scriptures have influenced tradition. Rarely do I hear a traditional message on burning in hell for all eternity. Meanwhile, books are published on this subject (some to defend the doctrine, others to challenge).

Truth and tradition are different. Truth is stable. Tradition is stubborn. Tradition appeals to carnal human reasoning. Jesus and Paul warned about tradition.

> **Making the word of God of none effect through your <u>tradition</u>, which ye have delivered: and many such like things do ye.** Mark 7:13

> **Beware lest any man spoil you through philosophy and vain deceit, after the <u>tradition</u> of men, after the rudiments of the world, and not after Christ.** Col. 2:8

Even though denominational leaders (Martin Luther, John Calvin and John Wesley) are born again, they are <u>not</u> error free or infallible. These errors flow into tradition. For some reason, God allows this. The perfect denomination does <u>not</u> exist. One denomination has it right here, but wrong there. For example, the Catholics have it right about marriage and contraceptives, while the Protestants allow divorce and contraceptives more freely. The traditional eternal retribution doctrine rings true in all but a few circles (Church of England and Seventh Day Adventist). We see dimly of God's throne of judgment and eternal retribution. Sometimes the smartest thing you can say is, "*I don't know.*" As one evangelist put it, "*I leave this all with the Lord.*"

Below is a fictional story for the purpose of illustration.

> A judge in Plainville, Texas had a precious son that he was very proud of. One summer, his son went deer hunting in Texas with a friend. The friend was from New York City and was <u>not</u> skillful with rifles. The friend accidentally dropped his rifle and the son was fatally wounded. The judge was very sorrowful and when asked what he was going to do, he said that he had a cell in the Plainville jail that was built for life long prisoners. The newspapers and television media picked up on this statement and presumptuously printed and proclaimed that the man from New York was going to spend all his days in the Plainville jail.
>
> When the man from New York was convicted of manslaughter the judge gave his sentence. He stated that he was very sorry that his son was taken from him and the maximum sentence for manslaughter in Texas was life in prison. However, he stated that because the newspaper, news media and almost everyone in town have put themselves in his place on his bench, he had decided to give the lightest sentence. The man from New York was sentenced to one day in jail!

One should be careful as pre-trial reporters before the Judge has given His verdict (see I Cor. 4:5). It is presumptuous and arrogant to speak as the Judge and pronounce endless suffering and torment, while staple words such as perish, consume and destruction are embedded in Scripture.

> **For now we see through a glass, darkly; but then face to face: now I know in part; but then shall I know even as also I am known.**
> I Cor. 13:12

Eternity is based upon a lack of understanding about time. This is really beyond our understanding. Some of His ways are past finding out. However, this is how I lean based on Scripture. Time deals with change. Jesus does <u>not</u> change. Jesus is the beginning and the end. Christians will be like Him and outside the effects and realm of time. Time is a resource like space and matter in this temporary environment. Time will be done away with (see Rev. 10:6). Eternity has connotations with time and therefore is a misnomer. The age will end. Judgment will be given. There is a day of the Lord or last day. There is a hell and there will be suffering "**for day and night,**" whatever that means (see Rev. 20:10). The suffering will end when God's judgment and wrath is satisfied. The suffering will probably end on the last day or the day of the Lord. His mercy endures forever, <u>not</u> His wrath (see Ezek. 16:42).

> **Behold, the <u>day of the LORD</u> cometh, cruel both with wrath and fierce anger, to lay the land desolate: and he shall <u>destroy</u> the sinners thereof out of it.** Isa. 13:9

> **The sun shall be turned into darkness, and the moon into blood, before the great and notable <u>day of the Lord</u> come:** Acts 2:20

This truth gives me comfort and sets me free from traditional religion. I have heard stories of individuals that have delved into the traditional teaching on eternity with harmful results. Anxiety and diseases are not the fruit of the Spirit of the Word. The truth makes you free.

> "The view that God is harsh and unforgiving, and that He will punish sinners with fire for ever and ever, has caused a great deal of anxiety and diseases related to anxiety. In extreme cases this view has led to insanity and even suicide."[7]

Christians would read their Bibles more if this doctrine were taught properly. The Catholic Church takes a cautious position on the "millennium," avoiding any absolute in order to avoid error. Let us hear both views. Not double minded, but a humble acknowledgement that the conclusion of an individual belongs to the Creator. Churches should avoid the pre-membership declaration of the eternal retribution for the unsaved. Christians would witness more. It was difficult for me to tell someone that they were going to burn in hell forever. Do you wonder why the Jehovah Witnesses are out knocking on doors? They do not have a fifty-pound doctrine to carry around (see Matt. 11:29).

Altar Call (Invitation)

The following is a typical altar call or invitation.

> "Everyone bow their heads and close their eyes with nobody looking around and nobody moving about. As the music softly plays, anyone who wants to make a decision to accept Jesus as their Savior please raise your hands real high so that I can see them. Pause. I see that hand. Is there another? Raise them high so that I can see them."

They have reversed it. The minister should be able to raise his hand and point out those whom the Spirit is dealing with (see John 6:64; Acts 8:26-39, 14:9, 26:28-29). Also, the decision is <u>not</u> whether we accept Jesus, but whether the Father has accepted us (see Rom. 12:1; Eph. 1:6; I Pet. 2:5).

> A poor peasant approached the gate of the king's palace. Two royal guards were standing guard. The peasant started to reach for the door to enter in. The guards stopped him. The peasant explained, "*Please, I have accepted the king as ruler. Let me enter.*" The guards laughed and replied, "*If you want to enter, the king must accept you. The king has sent out messengers with a royal coat. If anyone comes with a royal coat on, we will open the doors wide, without hesitation.*" (see Matt. 22:11)

Another popular invitation is to "*give your heart to Jesus*". Does giving your heart to Jesus add value to Jesus? They have reversed it. The Scripture says that He (Jesus) gives us His life and creates a new heart within us (see Matt. 20:28; Ezek. 36:26). After preaching the Word, one pastor reached out to a possible unsaved guest by reasoning with him or her whether they knew for sure they were going to heaven. The pastor reasoned that the attendant might say, "*I don't know for sure. I've been thinking about it.*" Scripture states that the preaching of the Word brings faith to believe, bypassing the thinking part of the soul, with an implantation of Holy Spirit and creation of a new nature. In others words, the pastor reversed it, you cannot think your way into salvation.

These reversals of the call of God to His elect are due to the free will philosophy, <u>not</u> Scripture.

Sit, Soak and Sour

Christian service is important, but I never understood the phrase "*sit, soak and sour*". This reverses a primary duty of the disciple. I prefer a "*sit, soak and shine*" phrase based upon the mountain top experience of Moses.

> **But when Moses went in before the LORD to speak with him, he took the veil off, until he came out. And he came out, and spake unto the children of Israel** *that* **which he was commanded. And the children of Israel saw the face of Moses, that the skin of Moses' face <u>shone</u>: and Moses put the veil upon his face again, until he went in to speak with him.** Exod. 34:34-35

If one is disobedient in his or her service, the phrase "*sit, soak and sin*" would be appropriate, but the value of Scripture meditation is paramount.

> *"As fundamental a step as we can take. . . is learning to meditate on Scripture— learning first to hear God's word, and let it inform and take root in us. This may be extremely difficult, for the churches have no courses on meditation, despite the fact that it is an art that must be learned from those who have mastered it, and despite the fact that the supreme task of the church is to listen to the Word of God."*
> Elizabeth O'Connor

Food

We should pray about what we should eat each day. Instead we reverse it by gathering whatever food we desire, whatever food we have a coupon for or whatever is on sale and then we ask God to bless it.

> **Give us day by day our daily bread.** Luke 11:3

Broken Heart

A Jewish inspiration story reads,

> "In a king's palace there are many chambers, and each door has its own particular key. But there is one implement, which can open all the doors, and that is— the ax. The kabbalistic kavanos are the keys to the gates in the World Above, each gate requiring its own particular kavanah— but a broken and humble heart can burst open all the gates and all the heavenly palaces."[8]

Man often looks negative upon a broken heart. God has reversed it to a positive.

The sacrifices of God *are* **a broken spirit: a broken and a contrite heart, O God, thou wilt not despise.** Ps. 51:17

Meanwhile, I disagree that God is broken hearted and unable to act and change the sinful deeds of man as some "free will" writers and speakers suggest. I disagree with denominations, churches and Christians who believe that praise will solve the issues of life. Consider your motive (see Matt. 15:8-9). Is your praise in order to mask sin or obtain a reward? Praise is acceptable, but not a solution to the issues of life or a cure for a broken heart. God accepts broken hearts.

Soul Winner

If you can text on a cell phone, surf the web or look up names and numbers in a phone book, you can use a Bible concordance. You do not need to know Hebrew or Greek to use a Bible concordance, but a concordance is necessary in order to determine what word(s) the English translators used. Moses and the apostles wrote and Jesus spoke truths about the soul of man that the English translators struggled to agree with their traditional views. Tradition can hide Truth in the English translations. For example, "soul" is translated "life" in Leviticus 17:11 and John 12:25. "Soulish" is translated "natural" in I Corinthians 15:44. The inspiration of some Scripture is an anomaly to mainstream Christianity. A disciple must continue in the Word underneath the hood of the high gloss of denominational vehicles (see John 8:31).

A child of God has the Spirit (Gr. *pnema*) of God (see Rom. 8:9). However, the soul can still manifest the old nature with sharp contention, intimidation or any other behavior similar to the unsaved (see Acts 15:39; Gal. 2:11-12; I Pet. 4:15). The soul (Gr. *psych*) of a child of God was not changed at new birth and could need a psychologist in order to correct behavior. A psychologist can be a soul winner. The soul of man is often incorrectly substituted to imply the Spirit of man or blended together with the Spirit of man. Scripture exhorts the salvation of the soul, but these apply to physical duration on earth, not birth into the kingdom of heaven. This is where the soul is incorrectly blended into the Spirit of man. The soul can sin. Therefore, Jesus died for the sins of the soul (see Rom. 6:6; Heb. 10:39). The sins of the soul are redeemed or paid for with the Blood of Jesus. The Spirit cannot sin (see I John 3:9). The soul is corrupt (see Eph. 4:22). The Spirit is incorrupt. At new birth salvation, only the Spirit of man is regenerated, not the soul (see John 3:5). Salvation is a new creation of the Spirit of man (see II Cor. 5:17). Meanwhile, the soul or the old man is not born again. After Spiritual salvation, the believer experiences joy, suffering and wrestling due to these two natures, the old and the new. The following is a diagram.

1) Spirit
    a. Before New Birth
        i. Dead or separated from God
        ii. Attached to the god of this world
    b. After New Birth (regenerated)
        i. New man in Christ

ii. Gift of Faith (Mind of Christ)
iii. Seal of Holy Spirit (sinless)
c. Can only be affected from heaven (New Birth)
d. Can <u>not</u> be won from earth

2) Soul
   a. Old man in Adam
   b. Mind (conscience, ability to repent)
   c. Will (sin, Blood of Jesus redeems)
   d. Emotion (crying, sorrow, pain, fear, happy, etc.)
   e. Can be affected or won from earth

3) Body
   a. Natural (earthly)
      i. Soul attached during earthly life
      ii. Corrupt blood from Adam
      iii. Soul separated from body at death
      iv. Resurrected
         1. Destroyed for un-saved
         2. Changed for regenerated
   b. Heavenly
      i. Flesh and bone
      ii. Able to exist in God's presence
      iii. No pain
      iv. Could resemble earthly at its best

The Lord recognizes value in leading or winning a soul from error, even when the new birth salvation is <u>not</u> on the table (see Jam. 5:19-20). Read the newspaper or listen to the news. Soul winners are needed everywhere.

A stronghold exists within Christendom that exalts the corrupt soul from Adam with an immortal existence. The immortality of the soul of man is based upon the transfer of assumed immortality when the Lord breathed into man's nostrils (see Gen. 2:7). However, this same divine breath is later referred to in Scripture to melt and consume (see Ezek. 22:21; Hag. 1:9). To exist permanently, man must eat of the fruit of the tree of life. Immortality was prevented when the Lord removed man from access to the fruit of the tree of life (see Gen. 3:22-24). The immortality of the soul was thought up with a junior high school bulling mentality in order to make room for another stronghold— never-ending conscious torment in hell (see II Cor. 10:4-5; I Tim. 6:16). Together, they become the familiar witnessing pseudo-key: "*Where you gonna spend eternity?*" The irony is thinking that a corrupt soul can produce a good choice toward a God the corrupt soul despises. Another irony happens when the so-called soul winner has his or her own soul damaged using the witnessing key. The witnessing key reverses into a witnessing barrier. One day I was in a Sears store when I hear a customer at the counter talking to the clerk. He sounded troubled and said that he had been told that he was going to spend eternity in hell. The clerk calmed him by saying that perhaps he would have better luck. My interpretation was that the Lord had just used a store clerk to calm a troubled soul from the witnessing key. The clerk was a soul winner. Once, I had a troubled time that was obvious to many. A Pentecostal preacher stood at a distance and said that he was praying for me, while a Baptist preacher remained at a distance also. Then one evening the Lord sent a tall African-American man to my door. He was a Jehovah's Witness. He listened to my troubled soul and gave me a word of encouragement. This man was a soul winner to me.

The fruit of the righteous *is* a tree of life; and he that winneth souls *is* wise. Prov. 11:30

The soul is the decision-making portion of a natural man that can act good or evil in the natural world. The soul can become chronically bent toward evil (see Gen. 6:5; Isa. 1:4-6). The soul can become faulty like any organ in the body that needs medicine. Medicine for the soul can be kind words that transition a disturbed soul to a tranquil soul within the natural world (see Gen. 50:15-21). A soul winner cannot be a person who leads someone to the Lord, because that is the work of the Spirit sent from the Father (see John 3:5, 6:44, 15:26). You could isolate on Andrew leading Peter to the Lord, but that was in a natural context, not a Spiritual (see John 1:40-42). The Spirit of man must be affected from heaven above, but the human soul (mind, will, intellect and emotion) can be affected from earth. This is called repentance.

Repentance is necessary to win a soul from ruin or physical death during this earthly life. Repentance is a decision and action from the soul of man that prolongs physical life (see Ezek. 18). There is nothing man can do to win anyone Spiritually, but the soul of man can be won from destructive behavior by speaking to the conscious. A soul winner is someone who leads someone away from a destructive lifestyle or a foolish decision (see Luke 12:16-21). This involves establishing boundaries, changing thoughts and medicine. However, a child may need a beating (see Prov. 23:14). All this takes wisdom on the part of the soul winner. Also, you can win your own soul through examination (see Luke 21:19). And the Lord can win your soul (see Jonah 4; Ps. 23:3). Usually a soul winner is another human(s).

Meanwhile, in direct contrast to wisdom, the Lord can use a foolish person to preach a foolish message to regenerate the Spirit (see I Cor. 1:21).

The following Scriptures are used in the further discussion about the soul of man.[9]

> **For the life** *(soul)* **of the flesh is in the blood:** Lev. 17:11a
>
> **It is sown a natural** *(soulish)* **body; it is raised a Spiritual body.** I Cor. 15:44a

Man was created from the dust of the earth. The soul of man was started when the Lord God breathed life into man. Moses wrote, "**The soul of the flesh is in the blood**" (Lev. 17:11a). Blood started flowing through the veins as the soul energized the flesh. When Adam and Eve ate of the fruit of the tree of good and evil, the fruit was digested and absorbed into the blood stream and corrupted the living soul with a sin nature. Still, the soul of the flesh was in the blood. Now the soul of man has a natural tilt toward returning to the dust of the earth and makes decisions that slowly or rapidly cause that return. A soul winner slows down the natural process. Consider stress from the soul, which increases blood pressure. The soul and blood are attached until separation at physical death. After physical death, the soul endures until judgment and can cry out to God (see Gen. 4:10; Rev. 6:10).

What saith the Scriptures (Rom. 4:3a)? There will not be natural souls and human blood in heaven because these are corrupt (see I Cor. 15:42, 50). In heaven, there will not be sorrow, crying and pain from the soul (see Rev. 21:4). There will not be fear from the soul (see Ps. 23:3-4; Rev. 21:8). When Paul went to the third heaven, he did not recognize himself because his soul was absent (see II Cor. 12:1-5). Souls will survive during the millennium reign, but will be changed or destroyed at judgment (see Rev. 20:4). The soul of man is the faulty decision-making part of man (see Joshua 24:19; Rom. 3:10-18). The soul is described as a natural body, which must be transformed into a Spiritual body. Paul wrote, "**It is sown a soulish body; it is raised a Spiritual body**" (I Cor. 15:44a). Toward the end of time, the soul is changed or annihilated. This is death or separation of the old man in order for the new man to inherit and enter the kingdom.

There was a cost for this change. The Lord requires payment for all violations against His law in order to maintain integrity (see I Cor. 15:56). Jesus gave His human soul as a ransom to remove the violations that His sheep commit (see John 10:15; Col. 2:14). His sheep do not hold onto their redeemed human souls because the soul of the sheep is transitioning to a permanent existence in a permanent abode (heaven). The sheep's redeemed soul will be changed from its corrupt nature to an incorruptible Spiritual body (see I Cor. 15:50-51). However, the unredeemed do hold onto or love their corrupt self-centered soul (see John 12:25). The unredeemed love making choices in this life, while the redeemed love saying "yes" to the Lord' choices (see II Cor. 1:19).

After His resurrection, Jesus described Himself as having flesh and bone, but no Blood (see Luke 24:39). The Blood of Jesus was offered on the altar in heaven (see Heb. 9:12). The human soul is associated with blood in order to atone for sins. Remember, the soul of the flesh is in the blood. The soul of a lamb contained a broad knowledge of good, but little or nil knowledge of evil. The blood of a lamb represented an earthly animal that did <u>not</u> make many faulty decisions, which made it suitable for representation. The Blood of Jesus came from His Father, <u>not</u> Adam. Jesus did <u>not</u> make faulty decisions or sin. Jesus suffered and died for the sins committed in the souls of His elect.

At judgment, Jesus will separate human Adamic souls from his or her newborn Spirit from God (see I Cor. 15:44; Heb. 4:12). Redeemed men and women will have the Spirit from God and a body of flesh and bone in heaven (see Rev. 21:3). Meanwhile, the unsaved will remain attached to their corrupt souls and will perish after judgment and punishment (see Matt. 10:28; John 12:25).

Since man inherited the corrupt soul of Adam, every man has the same corrupt nature. Be careful criticizing others. You are criticizing the same nature that exists within you. You would <u>not</u> criticize someone with a disease since the same possibility exists within you. The awful acts that you see others doing; the same seeds exist within yourself and everyone else (see Rom 2:1, 3:9). Just as a disease can return, so can the thoughts, words and deeds of the sinful nature. This includes Christian and non. This return does <u>not</u> affect the Spirit of the Christian, since the believer is sealed from separation (see Eph. 1:13). The Blood of Jesus will purge sins, but the nature of the soul remains corrupt.

Man cannot completely cure the soul. Man tries, through the department of corrections, but man cannot make absolute adjustments or connect conscious shortages to a stable platform because a stable platform (without regeneration) is missing in the soul of man (see Gen. 6:5; Jer. 17:9; Rom. 3:10-18). Since man cannot correct the soul and solve his failures, man entertains the idea that God is similar and unable to control the soul of man. Man rejects the analogy of a robot and assumes that God has given man free will and will never interfere with man's right to choose. Scripture disagrees and implies that God will interfere in rare times in order to prevent annihilation of the culture and to accomplish His will (see Gen. 6:7-8; Gal. 4:4).

All souls belong to the Lord and He judges them in righteousness. The righteous decisions and deeds from the soul of the Elect will be rewarded, while the meaningless decisions and deeds from the Elect are consumed in the fire (see I Cor. 3:13-15). The souls of the Elect of God will be changed or transformed (see I Cor. 15:51). This is a mystery that could involve destruction of the soul. Does God have to destroy the individual in order to create a robot?[10] Perhaps or something similar? The soul with its pride would covet in heaven. Souls would covet positions at Jesus' right and left hand, and at His feet. In heaven, the new creation from God will be the body, bone and Spirit, without the corrupt blood and soul from Adam.

This interpretation connects the dots at the liability of stepping on a stronghold of toes stuck in the concrete of tradition. When Jesus walked the earth, the Jewish leaders anticipated an earthly king. Today, Christian leaders anticipate soul winners to do the impossible (see Matt. 19:26). Ultimately, only the Lord God knows the full revelation of the soul.

Conclusion

These are a few examples that lean toward human reasoning. You may disagree. Some Christians need a different view in order to sustain a virtuous lifestyle, which is more important.

Chapter Seven

The Wiring and Currency of Denominations

A Christian denomination is an identifiable religious body under a common name, structure and doctrine. Denominations branch out into local churches. You should accept your local church's doctrine unless the pastor allows your disagreements. Then you can voice your disagreements, but you should not try to force your disagreements. You should be sensitive that your disagreements do not violate the conscience of others. Likewise, you should be sensitive that their doctrine does not violate your conscience. It is better to seek another denomination than to create disharmony or violate consciences. As Martin Luther (1483-1546) stated, "*I am bound by the Scriptures that I have quoted and my conscience is captive to the Word of God. I cannot and will not retract anything, since it is neither safe nor right to go against conscience.*"[1] Therefore, believers should be equally yoked with like-minded believers (see Phil. 2:2).

A hard case could be made that every Christian is required to understand the deep things of God. However, that does not seem to be. Every Christian should have discernment when teaching does not agree with his or her inner witness (see I John 2:20). Perhaps due to this inner witness, church attendance has decreased. Holy Spirit may put a believer to sleep during a church service to prevent him or her from hearing incorrect teaching. Holy Spirit led me to avoid one meeting where the visiting evangelist incorrectly implied that Jephthah sacrificed his daughter on the altar of God (see Jud. 11:29-40). I later heard the tape message and the evangelist acknowledged that scholars disagreed, but I was the only one who believed that the daughter was dedicated to virginity, <u>not</u> a burnt sacrifice.

Beware and be wise. The Father said to listen to Jesus. There is <u>not</u> a man or woman on the face of the earth that you can trust like the Word of God. My desire is to know and hear the Truth. I learned that I could <u>not</u> trust denominations to interpret the Word of God correctly in all major areas. I had to pray and study the Word for myself. Still, it is good to study how other denominations believe and why. Your denomination might <u>not</u> tell you how others believe. Denominations are correct in most areas, while incorrect in others. Denominations disagree with each other. A common denominator within all denominations is that they believe they have the whole truth. Each denomination believes they are the hundred-dollar bills, but many only add up to fifty. All denominations have limited truth. Key words such as faith, elect and perish are skewed in order to satisfy consciences due to a lack of conviction to honor the Word. Why do they do this? The sovereign Lord has barred their understanding in order to scatter them into separate camps.

As a student of the Word, I struggle with denominations. Some violate my conscience that I inherited from Adam, while others disturb my Spirit from Jesus. Tradition within a denomination is like rotten wood within a structure of Stone and people avoid a structure with rotten wood. Each denomination is similar to an hourglass. The sand is correct doctrinal teaching. The air is traditional beliefs, human reasoning or error. Each hourglass leans this way or that. The sand is the foundation but the air exists also. For example, one denomination may be liberal in doctrine but strong in grace. Another may be strong in doctrine but weak in mercy toward others. No hourglass exists that is completely full of sand or error free.

The good news is that God had given His Word and His Spirit. Heed the words of the Father about the Son, "**Hear Him**" (see Luke 9:35). The Words of Jesus is Truth. Man can err. The problem is when you read Scripture and voice your concerns to a denominational leader or member; they honor their traditions because denominations expect conformity. Individuals are drawn to denominations believing they have experienced the fullness of truth. If ever the fingerprints of God are visible, it is seen in the vessels of denominations.

New denominations were established when God moved on individuals and his or her current denomination did not approve. Remember, Jesus was rejected because He did not come from the established religious channel or from an accredited geographical location. Meanwhile, the common Jewish man or woman saw the beautiful temple and the long robes of their leaders while hearing their long prayers. The visuals from their religion were impressive. They thought their leaders had it right. Yet Jesus of Nazareth established Christianity and the beautiful temple in Jerusalem was destroyed.

Denominations within Christianity have a slight tendency to sway toward the approval of man and overlook the authority of God (see Gal. 1:10). This centers in the realm of **control**, between the comforts of a religion versus the challenges of the Kingdom (see I Sam. 8:7). Apostolic succession is one of the ultimate control thoughts, which states that Jesus choose the apostles and a daisy chain sequence of approval must follow to be legitimate. Christianity does not have a Spiritual channel that is single-threaded through history. Jesus directs from heaven into individual hearts regardless of earthly denominational ties through history. Consider that the Christian church experienced a few major schisms in the first sixteen centuries. At times, the Catholic Church was very powerful and controlling. The Pre-Reformation period (1215-1515) started challenging the supreme control of the Catholic Church.[2] The Protestant denominations started when the

Protestant Reformation (1516-1563) moved away from the Catholic Church.

What are the differences within Protestant denominations? Many of the denominations were determined based upon the five points of Arminianism and the five counterpoints of Calvinism. These points were debated in 1618 at Dordt in the Netherlands and the debate continues today.

Arminianism (named after James Arminius 1560-1609)

1) Free will consists of the human ability to choose good over evil: man has the power to cooperate with God's grace or resist it.
2) Conditional election is determined by human choice of God; not God's choice of individuals. God's election is determined by foreseen faith in individual human choice of Him.
3) Universal redemption or general atonement is available for all to be saved, but is effective only to those who choose to accept it.
4) Resisting grace for salvation is possible.
5) Falling from grace after salvation is possible.

Calvinism (named after John Calvin 1509-1564; also called Reformed theology; direct opposition to each point above)

1) Man is totally deprived of the ability to choose God unless Holy Spirit regenerates man. Man can choose in the natural realm, but not the Spiritual.
2) Man is unconditionally elected based upon God's choice and not upon any individual merit or human choice since all are totally deprived in the Spiritual realm.
3) The cross provided definite atonement for the sins of His elect. The atonement was precise based upon the intent of the Father. This point was difficult for me at first due to my Baptist background. The reformers, not John Calvin, established this point.
4) The grace of God is irresistible to those He regenerates.

5) The regenerated saints will persevere. Salvation cannot be renounced with the natural mind or will of man.

Scholars cannot defeat Calvinism due to support from Scripture, while Arminianism continues from rational support due to the familiar experience of personal choices in the natural world.

Additionally, the Reformation included five tenants of:

- Scripture alone,
- For the glory of God alone,
- Salvation by Christ's work alone,
- Salvation by grace alone,
- And justification by faith alone.

Since then, many Protestant denominations have moved back toward parts of Arminianism, placing the burden on the sinner to "do something" to initiate salvation and to "continue doing something" in order to continue in a state of grace. This is similar to the Catholic Church's original model. However, due to the Reformation, the Catholics have abandoned obvious Scripture err to suppress additional departures.

To understand denominations, you need to understand the above five points of Arminianism and Calvinism. These points are critical in determining the Protestant denominations.

Catholics are basically Armenian and receive the life of faith through the church. I agree with the Catholic's definition of faith as a gift from God as opposed to many Protestants' definition of faith as a natural attribute of man. Also, the Catholics are closer to the Scripture toward marriage and communion. The Catholics are more serious about these two doctrines, which they consider sacraments. Catholics believe that communion nourishes the body of Christ. I agree. Meanwhile, Protestant culture after salvation leans more toward what I can do for Christ, versus what Christ can do for me. Protestants observe communion less often, sometimes 3 or 4 times a year. Liberal Protestant denominations observe communion regularly. Liberals see their need for forgiveness. Legalistic Protestant denominations observe communion rarely. The main purpose of communion is a remembrance of what Christ did (see Luke 22:19). The Catholics are closer to Scripture concerning marriage. The Catholics state that God does not recognize a marriage that does not have the intent to bear children. The Catholics do not recognize contraceptives and no acts on self. Contraceptives violate God design for procreation. I agree and believe that Protestants are more liberal toward marriage and procreation. I worked with a Catholic from Long Island, NY. He told me of working in Greenville, SC and his desire to go out for a social drink with his Protestant co-workers. The Protestants refused because they practiced Christian abstinence from alcohol. He voiced a bit of hypocrisy. His co-workers were divorced and remarried two or three times, while he honored God with one wife for life. I thought about the Protestants I knew that were divorced. Taking your wife out for a social drink once a week would be better than allowing it to end in divorce court.

Concerning **church government**, the New Testament recognizes the office of apostle, prophet, evangelist, pastor, teacher, elder, bishop and deacon. Most churches lack a New Testament model where the pastor is a shepherd to the congregation, while a bishop is an overseer (see Eph. 4:11; I Tim 3:1-7). God appoints a pastor, while the church appoints a bishop. Paul, the apostle, wrote to Timothy, the pastor, guidelines for appointing bishops and deacons (see I Tim. 3:1-10). Should you do whatever the pastor asks you to do? You should do whatever Jesus asks you to do. Jesus can speak through the pastor; therefore you should seriously consider what the pastor is requesting. If you have a reason for not doing what is requested, let the pastor know (see Heb. 13:17). The pastor is a shepherd, not a dictator over your faith (see II Cor. 1:24). Some members are able to do whatever the pastor asks, deacons for example. The pastor can incorrectly infer that all members have this calling. Meanwhile, Jesus set an example of leadership by washing the disciple's feet (see

John 13:1-17). Incredibly, Jesus said that the Father would do whatever we ask (see John 15:16, 16:23).

Often the overseer(s) are the deacons, elders, church counsel and/or the pastor. Nevertheless, the church is effective when the leaders are plugged into the will of the Lord. From observation, most churches have a functional church government.

Four other doctrines are:

Young Earth creation: The earth is between 6000 - 10,000 years old based upon the Scripture's genealogy record. This agrees with the evidence of science. In contract, evolution and the old-earth-age estimates entertain the creative reasoning and satisfy the conscience of the natural mind.

Gifts of Holy Spirit: All the gifts of Holy Spirit are in operation today and were not limited to the 1st century apostles.

Conditional immortality: The unsaved will perish or be annihilated after the judgment and the wrath of God is satisfied— probably in one day of wrath (see Isa. 13:9; Rom. 2:5). Day and night will end (see Rev. 20:10). Only the saved will obtain immortality and continue to exist (see I Cor. 15:42-54).

Christian Perfection: This doctrine is not a sinless fixed nature in this current world, but a mature state that exercises victory over sin before physical death. I find common ground with John Wesley (Methodism) here. Perfection is not a prerequisite of salvation. Christian perfection follows redemption by the Blood of Jesus and regeneration by Holy Spirit. Christian perfection is a high mark of a disciple and the final state of sanctification in heaven.

These Christian doctrines are important and separate denominations into Baptists, Catholics, Lutherans, Methodists, Presbyterians, Pentecostals, Seventh Day Adventists,

Anglicans and many more. Denominations are fine. Few would like to sit in a church that preaches doctrines that violates his or her conscience toward Scripture.

My personal beliefs favor:

- Five point Calvinism,
- Young earth creation,
- All the gifts of Holy Spirit for today,
- And conditional immortality.

To elaborate, I believe that God initiates salvation regardless of the will of man. Man is unable or total deprived of the ability to choose God. Hearts are darkened and human wills are in bondage to sin. Consider that no groups of protestors exist that cries out to the injustice of his or her inability to choose God, but rather the opposite; they desire to eliminate any trace of God. How God chooses His elect is beyond our ability to understand (see Mark 4:26-27). We should understand that His choice is <u>not</u> based upon any merit found in the individual (see Rom. 9:11). I believe the age of the earth to be around 6,000 years old. The original earth was much better prior to the flood during Noah's time with a higher oxygen content and less radiation from the sun due to a water vapor canopy around the near atmosphere, which blessed the observer with a beautiful array of colors that resembled our post flood rainbow (see Chapter 10). Before the flood, the environment was friendlier to life; man lived longer and was healthier. Vegetables grew in abundance, while animals flourished to great size and quantity. The flood created the abundant coal and oil supplies under the earth from the plant and animal burials. The science that observes natural occurrences, I accept. I reject the theories that draw conclusions by reversing those occurrences: evolution and the old age of the earth. I reject the belief that parts of the gifts of Holy Spirit ended with the death of the last apostle. I reject the belief in the immortality of the soul. I believe that immortality is reserved for the elect. I interpret **"perish," "destruction"** and "**consume**" literally. The unsaved will be judged based upon his or her conscious words and deeds, thrown into the lake of fire and annihilated after the judgment and wrath of God is satisfied. They shall be as though they had not been (Obad. 1:16).

Most of my Christian life I have been a member of a Southern Baptist church, but I have visited and joined other denominations. Godly Christians are in these denominations. Still, I would like to point out some disagreements. If I were to write about my agreements, the list would be long. Therefore, I limit the list to a few disagreements. My goal is not to be an accuser of the brethren. My goal is to reveal that incorrect doctrine affects behavior. Christians that fit well in their churches may not understand my struggles. My struggles may be a calling from God, to testify of error.

Church of God (Gifts of Holy Spirit)

Do you look for and recognize the work of Holy Spirit in a Christian's life or do you look for and recognize the work the Christian has done (see II Cor. 5:12)? Is it more important to see what God has done in the Christian's heart or is it more important to see what the Christian has done? A simple answer: works do not beget holiness (see I Tim. 4:12-16).

I was a member of an Armenian Church of God for almost three years. The church has a wonderful ministry to the poor and homeless that is right in line with the gospels. I agree with the gifts of Holy Spirit for today, so I believed this church was where I belonged. However, I would feel a bit uncomfortable when they would come to the altar and emulate past days of the moving of Holy Spirit. Mostly, I would sit in church and feel the peace and security of God.

From observation, I learned that Armenians are work oriented. Not salvation by works, but performance based. They imply that God has done everything He is going to do, so now you need to get going (cf. Isa. 40:31). If an Armenian does not see visible works in another Christian, they have an "*I don't need you*" attitude (see I Tim. 5:25). I remember the senior pastor making a visible appearance in my Sunday school class to recognize the teacher's role as a volunteer on a weekend. The senior pastor did not say anything; he just stood in front beside the teacher to give him a little praise. The teacher looked a bit uncomfortable. Other times, individuals were recognized from the pulpit for his or her God called and anointed ministry. However, when it came time to recognize the senior pastor for his thirty-five years of ministry, he would not come out. The church board had to vote him to appear. This vote was announced to the congregation. Then they did a fine visual presentation of reviewing his service for God. Later, I wondered if he resisted in order to intensify his recognition. I could not understand why he was adamant about recognizing others, but not himself.

Then I noticed lifestyle issues, such as pregnancy out of wedlock. Another young lady from an onstage ministry would appear multiple times at the altar in a repentant attitude with different boyfriends. The church leaders appeared to look the other way: perhaps due to the stronghold of current culture. However, I came to church to get away from the natural ways of the world, not see them on display (see I Tim. 5:20). The solution for lifestyle issues is marriage, abstinence or excommunication. Instead of a solution, it appeared that acceptance was based upon what they did in ministry. However, if you want to win the city for Jesus, you need to start with sanctification (cf. Rom. 12:1).

Then the senior pastor gave me a "question mark" stare from across the room. I did not know how to interpret the stare since he did not say anything. I prayed and wanted to stay, but I felt led to move on. Also my conscience was bothered by some of their teaching. For example, implying that Jesus did not have a clue when He went to the cross if anyone would be saved! It was no longer the place for me.

From my experiences with a few Armenian churches, I have learned they tolerate sinful lifestyles as long as they see ministry results. This may stem from their free will doctrines.

Armenians believe they can win the city for Jesus. Armenians believe Spiritual salvations are contingent upon personal initiatives and financial resources. Their objectives are in their name based upon their recognition of their efforts. These beliefs have partial Scriptural support, but neglect the unconditional moving of the Arm of God, regardless of the efforts and resources of men. However, they do believe and practice most Scriptural principles.

Presbyterian Church (Calvinism)

Next, I visited a Presbyterian Church in America for several weeks. I agree with Calvinism or Reformed doctrine. I thought, "*This is where I belong.*" Someone warned me, "*John, Presbyterians are snobs.*" I am not judging the Presbyterians, but only writing what someone said and what happened at the Presbyterian Church. The Presbyterians have a congregational prayer of confession that contains Scriptural truth about God, mixed with human failures that may or may not be true for everyone in the congregation. For example:

> "We confess we remain captive to doubt and fear, bound by the ways that lead to death. We overlook the poor and the hungry, and pass by those who mourn; we are deaf to the cries of the oppressed, and indifferent to calls for peace; we despise the weak, and abuse this good earth you entrusted to us."

I did not feel comfortable confessing this. I believe this can get into your thinking and lead to similar behavior. These confessions were going in the wrong direction. Instead of putting off the old man, they were putting on the old man (see Eph. 4:22; Col. 3:9).

Most members were polite, but as the weeks went by, I noticed suspicion from some members because I was single. Did they want to call me out and see where I stood? One

Sunday night an elderly gentleman came up beside me, made a hand gesture and said, *"This is where you get your pay check from."* Then after a Wednesday night discussion, another member coupled my name with another man's name and gave me the left-handed handshake while the elderly gentleman was off to the side with a disgusted look. Could this be their way to vent their frustration toward denominations that accept gay membership and ordain gay ministers? John Calvin writes, *"some dogs bark out."*[3] I did not understand their motive; perhaps it was a bit of hazing before membership or they could have made a congregational confession that affected their behavior. They could have been nurturing their narcissism since one of my accusers appeared competitive and my knowledge of Scripture may have been intimidating (see Acts 6:10-11). In postmodernism, perception is reality, yet Scripture cautions against devising wicked imaginations, sewing discord and bearing a false witness (see Exod. 20:16; Prov. 25:18). I considered calling one of my accusers privately by telephone, but decided they were longtime Presbyterians and I no longer felt comfortable becoming part of their group. Perhaps I should jump for joy (see Luke 6:22-23). I concluded that God had given me a warning from someone for a reason (see II Tim. 3:5). Overall, Presbyterians are solid Christians.

Concerning homosexuality, science proves that same-sex unions are not according to design or according to the theory of evolution.[4] Scripture states that homosexuality is contrary to nature and is an abomination toward God (see Rom. 2:26-27; Lev. 18:22). Those who practice it will not inherit the kingdom of God (see Gal. 5:19-21). I wish this were not a part of the fallen nature, although pride may be a greater sin (see Prov. 16:5; John 19:11). Meanwhile, adultery is more widespread and more detrimental to the culture.

Nevertheless, if I was a homosexual and I walked into the church of the Lord Jesus Christ, I hope I would find deliverance. In the gospels, Jesus and His disciples cast out unclean spirits (see Matt. 10:1). The American church has evolved into a model that expects large involvement from members, but possesses little ability to deliver and equip. This is due to a saturation of free will and a denial of control from God. Churches want to admire and use you, but appear passive in fixing you (cf. Matt. 11:5).

Seventh Day Adventist (conditional immortality)

The apostle John exhorts believers to try the spirits or in my case to determine what denomination the Lord has assigned to me (see I John 4:1). Next, I visited a Seventh Day Adventist church for several weeks. I liked their low-key attitude. Humble Christians have a calming influence. I agree with their conditional immortality doctrine. Yet it seems every denomination has a common carnal story that entertains and validates their beliefs. I heard one too many stories about worshipping on Saturday; such as when a Baptist minister that once was the president of a Bible college and had pastored a church for thirty years, etc., but when confronted with the question as to why the Sabbath was changed to Sunday, the Baptist minister looked dumbfounded and unable to find anything in his Bible to support why he worshipped on Sunday! Adventists make a strong Scriptural case for worshipping on the Sabbath, but it starts to break down when they tie the mark of the beast in Revelation 14:9-12 with Protestants, Catholics and pagans that worship on Sunday. Adventists believe they keep the commandments mentioned in verse 12 by Sabbath day worship. This is their private interpretation. I believe Jesus initiated the transition away from the Sabbath. He was criticized for working on the Sabbath and He did not deny He was not working. He said that He was the Lord of the Sabbath and the Sabbath was made for man, not the other way around. From Acts 20:7 where the apostles came together on the first day of the week (Sunday) and the below Scripture not to judge, whether right or wrong, the Sabbath, I was convinced they were wrong.

> **Let no man therefore judge you in meat, or in drink, or in respect of an holyday, or of the new moon, or of the sabbath** *days*: Col. 2:16

The Adventists' extreme Sabbath and Armenian teaching and their favorite word being "*choice*" and their loathing of "*predestination*," led me to move on. One fine elder said that he would not serve a God that chooses one person over another. Man does have limited choice in the natural realm, but God makes all the choices in the Spiritual. Still, they are so right about conditional immortality and the annihilation of the unsaved.

Conclusion

Denominations may reference a Scripture here or there, while the majority of the Scriptures may contradict their doctrinal statements. They are locked into their denominational view. Why? The classic Armenian/Calvinism debate is an example. The Armenian Christians believe you place yourself in a state of grace and can walk out of grace. The Calvinist Christians believe God places you in a state of grace that is irresistible to walk away from. Someone is wrong. Both cannot be right. I believe the Spirit of God has allowed blindness to certain parts of the Scripture in order to create denominations in order to prevent unity of all Christians so that they do not use their combined influence similar to the Catholic Church's rule prior to the Reformation. A majority as large as the Church speaking as one voice would force their influence on others. The corrupt soul from Adam is still a part of regenerated Spiritual Christians. Therefore, they have been programmed like robots locked into various camps of interpretations to march forward (see Luke 1:51). An Armenian cannot change his stripes to believe that God chooses one sinner over another; nor can a Calvinist believe that a sinner can resist the grace of God. God establishes the camps (see Matt. 16:18). This answers a lot of questions. I could be wrong. I cannot prove it. One day the earth shall be filled with the knowledge of the glory of the LORD, as the waters cover the sea, but currently we see dimly, including denominations toward the full revelation of God's truths (see Hab. 2:14).

Being a student of the Word reveals many things, including the observation of the vainglory of man, but also the capacity for obedience to the glory of God. In an environment where obedience flourishes and where salvations, healings and miracles are credited to God alone, a church or denomination can be an influence for the Kingdom of God. It would be interesting to see how the denominational world would respond to an apostle or prophet sent by God. <u>Not</u> an apostle or prophet appointed by man, but an apostle or prophet sent by God. Would he or she be rejected? Perhaps the greatest criticism would come from the Christian community. Hopefully, he or she would be received and our nation would be blessed. I predict a move of God within small group settings away from the eyes of the world and the worldwide media. There is a struggle when too much attention is given. Double mindedness can occur in avoiding the vainglory of man and acknowledging the glory of God. This may be why miracles occur in third world countries that are without the modern media spotlight on the works of men.

Please note that I am aware of my personal failures in the above circumstances and the challenges that ministers face in the good fight of faith (see Jam. 5:16).

Chapter Eight

Gospel Robots

The preaching of the gospel or evangelism is all about Jesus. Salvation is contingent upon God. Salvation is impossible with man. Therefore, Jesus should be the only One to receive praise for salvation. You do not praise water for satisfying thirst. The evangelists that Jesus sends into His harvest are just doing what is expected (see Luke 17:10).

Therefore:

- **No evangelism happens unless Jesus starts it.**
- **No one understands what is happening except Jesus.**
- **No one questions genuine salvations when they happen.**
- **No one should receive praise except Jesus.**

It is easy to believe that everything Christians do should lead to salvation for the unsaved. I get excited in the anticipation of seeing lives changed. Still, no matter how much emphasis toward this goal is applied, Christians cannot "make it happen".

> **Not that we are sufficient of ourselves to think any thing as of ourselves; but our sufficiency *is* of God; Who also hath made**

us able ministers of the new testament; not of the letter, but of the spirit: for the letter killeth, but the spirit giveth life. II Cor. 3:5-6

Christians hold video slide presentations of world population versus Christian population. They develop strategies to reach demographics. They raise financial aide toward targeted areas. They gather in large arenas for prayer and to share concerns. These things are fine, but if the Lord Jesus Christ does not extend His hand, nothing Spiritual will happen (see Acts 11:21). Man can do many things in the natural realm, but Jesus controls the Spiritual.

Simple theology takes Scripture out of context and implies that "**whosoever shall call upon the Name of the Lord shall be saved**" (Rom. 10:13). In context, it is God that sends the evangelist to those He has predestined to call upon the Name of the Lord.

Nevertheless:

- Christians have a genuine concern for the unsaved.
- Christians believe they can make evangelism happen.
- Christians establish unscriptural strategies to "make it happen".
- Christians blame themselves and others when it does not happen.
- Christians praise themselves and others when it does happen.

The word "*evangelism*" is not found in the King James Version of the Bible. The word "*evangelist(s)*" is found three times and means "*a preacher of the gospel*". The word "*gospel*" from the same root as "*evangelist*" is found seventy-seven times and means "*good news*". The word "*witness*" means "*testimony or martyr*". The Greek word "*martyr*" means "*one who dies for his faith*", because that was commonly the price of witnessing. Martyrdom is a scriptural cause of death.

The word "*apostle*" means "*he that is sent, representative, messenger, envoy*".

The contemporary belief is that every Christian is called to be an evangelist or witness. I do not dispute the witness role, because everyone is a witness whether they want the role or not. I dispute the evangelist role. Pastors exhort their congregation to witness. Yet I do not see the members obeying. Can it be that God has not called them to be an evangelist, a preacher of the gospel? The pastor has put the message in his or her head, but has God put the calling in their heart? I am not anti-evangelistic, but some Christians can be obedient to the Lord and never be on the scene, when a salvation occurs. I have been out witnessing with Christians that have no desire to preach the gospel to others. Others, including myself, might share the gospel with no results, except maybe to impress our friends. I desire a correct doctrine of evangelism that does not place guilt on the Christian if they are never on the scene to experience a salvation and not to praise Christians and jeopardize a stumbling block for others, when a salvation does happen.

Most of the evangelism that I have experienced was based upon the premise that man has the ability to initiate the salvation event. This is due to a misinterpretation of repentance. Repentance is a change of mind and is an act that man can do.

> **I indeed baptize you with water unto repentance: but he that cometh after me is mightier than I, whose shoes I am not worthy to bear: he shall baptize you with the Holy Ghost, and** *with* **fire: Matt. 3:11**

John the Baptist was able to recognize repentance by men. Repentance has visual results. However, salvation is a change of nature that only God can do. The unsaved can repent as well as the saved (see Matt. 27:3; Rev. 2:5). Repentance does not change one's nature. Consider that the entire gospel of John does not mention repentance even in the ministry of John the Baptist (see John). Jesus came preaching repentance before the new birth conversion was available in order to change the culture. Man can repent without salvation (see Matt. 3:11). Salvation is receiving the Spirit of God. When salvation occurs, repentance will follow. Repentance is one of the works that verify saving faith (see Jam. 2:20). Christian repentance is a pathway to perfection, not salvation. Christian perfection is similar to a robot of Jesus, not exactly like a robot, but closer to a robot than a free agent. Repentance is living how we were designed to live by God that sustains life. Repentance is living by the holy law of God.

> **Now when they heard** *this*, **they were pricked in their heart, and said unto Peter and to the rest of the apostles, Men** *and* **brethren, what shall we do? Then Peter said unto them, Repent, and be baptized every one of you in the name of Jesus Christ for the remission of sins, and ye shall receive the gift of the Holy Ghost.** Acts 2:37-38

Must you repent and be baptized in order to be saved? No. These acts follow salvation. A newborn Christian may ask, "What must I do to be saved?" because his or her carnal mind has not been renewed (see Acts 16:30). Suppose a couple adopts a seven-year-old boy and the child asks, *"What must I do to be part of this family?"* The couple corrects and comforts the young child by saying, *"The first thing you must do is to change your thinking. You are part of this family, but we need a lawyer to change your name."* After salvation, repentance is a change of thinking and baptism is identification with the Name of Jesus. Due to the misinterpretation of repentance as a prerequisite to salvation, man's efforts are the focus. This leads to hardball religion that emphasizes how serious the rejection of Jesus is, such as, *"there is not a hell hot enough or an eternity long enough for any one who rejects Christ."*[1]

Please beware of the many fearful caricatures out there. You cannot think your way to a change of nature.

> **Then saith he unto his disciples, The harvest truly *is* plenteous, but the labourers *are* few; Pray ye therefore the Lord of the harvest, that he will send forth labourers into his harvest.**
> Matt. 9:37-38

    Another manmade method is visual or through the physical sense of sight. This is framed as being a good witness or showing the unsaved you have something they do not. Yes, Christians are to be a witness to what the Lord has done in his or her heart, but not to bait the unsaved with what they have, such as material things. The unsaved are watching Christians in order to accuse them, not to be like them. Observe the example of the apostle Paul who suffered much for the cause of Christ (see II Cor. 11). Paul had joy and contentment, but not a lifestyle that many wanted. Still, Christians exhort, "You may be the only Jesus people ever see." Well, many people saw Jesus, but believing in Him is Spiritual regeneration within the heart, not an experience with the sense of sight. Jesus was marred to visual horror. Therefore, faith is the means of salvation, not eye candy (see Heb. 11:1). Christians are salt and light to the world in order to sustain the culture (see Matt. 5:13-16). The conscience of the unsaved reacts in a culture where Christians live by faith. This is the value of witnessing — it sustains life in the natural. However, the spirit of the unsaved must be Spiritually regenerated in order to enter the Spiritual Kingdom.

    The harvest belongs to the Lord. Man cannot influence God through intellect. Only Jesus has the power to save. Evangelism is started by the Lord sending laborers into His harvest to foolishly (based upon the intellect of man) preach the gospel (see I Cor. 1:18-21). This truth is observable. Why are Christians not evangelizing in Saudi Arabia? God has not sent evangelists to Saudi Arabia. This is a contemporary example of how God sends evangelists and <u>not</u> man. Nevertheless, there is a small Christian election from God in Saudi Arabia (see Acts 17:26). Still, religions other than Islam are prohibited even for expatriate Christian gatherings.[2] If God wills a door would be opened in Saudi Arabia. I have known Christians that have gone on missionary trips that were scheduled by man with little or no results. I have known and read of missionaries that have gone on missionary trips scheduled by God with incredible results (see II Cor. 2:14). I have observed the pride of man concerning evangelism. The pride of man can be vainly credited for evangelism. This is illustrated by the following fictitious story.

The Brazilian church

One summer, a man named John visited his cousin in Brazil. The Brazilian church where his cousin attended was praying that the Lord would send workers into His harvest to add to the church. One evening while John was relaxing with his cousin, he heard a scream. Without thinking he ran to help. John had forgotten that it was dangerous to go out after dark. He identified the scream from a nearby hut and shouted, "*What's wrong*?" A woman came out and said her daughter was choking on a carrot. John, knowing the Heimlich maneuver, helped the young girl to expel the carrot. The family was relieved and John had an opportunity to witness to the family. John was surprised when they were saved. The following Sunday morning the family came to church with John and his cousin. The pastor announced their salvation and everyone praised the Lord.

The following week as John was alone and returning home from work, three men stopped him. They demanded his cash. He handed it over without hesitation. As they were leaving, John noticed the leader was about his size and offered him his shirt. They were pricked in the heart. Again, the three men were saved and met John and his cousin at the Brazilian church. This continued for five weeks. John would meet someone, a group or a family, share the gospel and they would show up in church.

The fifth Sunday was different. One lady raised her hand until the pastor had her attention. The pastor tried to ignore her, but she was relentless. Finally, he said, *"Dear lady, what is so important?"* She said, *"John from my village has been responsible for these salvations as well. You have never mentioned his name!"* The pastor replied, *"John, who is John, he is an unprofitable servant of the Lord that has done what was required of him. This is the work of the Lord and He deserves all the honor and glory for these salvations."* With that, the Lord continued to use John, his servant, each week.

In the fall, John returned home to America. What an experience of seeing precious lives saved for the glory of God. On his third day home as he was approaching his apartment complex's mailbox, he noticed an elderly man walking up to him. John started talking about the weather and the man said he was just glad to be breathing one more day. This led John to share the gospel and the man was saved. And about an hour later his wife was saved. John was so surprised. The same thing was happening in America! That Sunday the elderly man and his wife went to church with John. The couple went forward at the invitation to announce the change they had experienced the following week. The pastor was quick to ask who shared the gospel with them. They relied, *"John from our apartment complex."* The pastor asked John to stand and everyone was excited that the Lord had used John in this way.

This continued every week. John would be out and about and someone, a group or a family would be saved. Afterwards, they would come to church to make it public. Once during a service the pastor asked, *"John, how many souls did you bring with you to church today?"* Then the pastor frowned at the congregation and said, *"How come the rest of you cannot witness like John? This church would be packed."*

Soon a local Christian television station heard about John. In order to share what the Lord was doing, John went to be interviewed. The station manager told John that souls were what they were all about. John did not feel comfortable when he shared his story. The audience seemed to be clapping at him.

Eventually, John no longer felt comfortable attending his church. He would visit other churches, bringing with him folks that had been saved the previous week. John would humbly request to the pastor not to mention his name. John's request would be ignored and the congregation would know how the Lord was using John. John was asked to meet with the senior pastor and staff of a large church in town. They wanted John to hold workshops at the church to teach the staff his methods. John was thankful for their desire for the unsaved, but he was not comfortable teaching because he was more of a learner than a teacher. John stated that Jesus was his Trainer. As John was about to leave they offered him a position at the church as their minister of evangelism. John declined even after their handsome salary offer.

John remembered how content he was in the Brazilian church. He missed being united as one, giving glory and praise to the Lord alone for these precious lives. And he remembered how the Brazilian pastor had said that glorifying Jesus was what they were all about.

Then it ended. John went a whole week without an opportunity to share the gospel. What had happened? Suddenly the phone rang. It was his cousin in Brazil. "*Cousin Johnny, cousin Johnny*" the voice shouted. "*It has happened to me, like it happened to you. This week three people were saved and I was there. They are coming to church this Sunday. We haven't had a salvation in the church since you returned to America.*"

(see Matt. 6:13b, 9:38; I Cor. 3:5; Luke 17:10; John 3:8; Rom. 10:15)

Contentment

Are you content with the will of the Lord? Christian contentment is the acceptance of a higher standard. Contentment is not apathy or inactivity. John the Baptist struggled with contentment (see Matt. 11:2). The apostle Paul learned contentment (see Phil. 4:11). The will of the Lord should bring contentment. Often the will of the Lord disagrees with personal preference or free will. The will of Paul was for the salvation of the Jews (see Rom 10:1). However, he avoided the Jews due to the will of God.

Family Life

Free will dominates the American family. The free will view of salvation can disrupt contentment within a family. This is illustrated by the following fictitious story.

> A Christian couple (William and Mary) have two children. Their daughter, Susan is a Christian. Their son, David is not a Christian. The couple is devoted to the Lord and strives to live a life pleasing to Him. They pray daily for their children, but their attitude about evangelism will affect their relationship with their children.
>
> Free will: The couple is pleased with Susan's decision to accept Christ as her Savior. The couple is struggling with David. They want him saved but David has not yet accepted Christ as his Savior. The burden is on David. There is tension between the couple and their unsaved son to accept Christ. Sometimes they confront him about it. Other times, they show their silent disappointment in a subtle way. David knows his parents love him. But he also senses their disappointment and is frustrated that they do not understand his inability to convert himself or to co-operate with the grace of God.
>
> Sovereign will: The couple is thankful for the grace He has shown to Susan. The couple is

praying that the Lord will show the same grace to David. They realize that God is sovereign and David is unable to convert himself. They love David and accept God's will, whether David is saved or remains unsaved. Their relationship is the same with both children.

Does sovereign will imply that David cannot be saved? No. Sovereign will means that David cannot "make it happen". Meanwhile, his parents and sister are to love the Lord more than themselves and David (see Luke 14:26). David's family is to do what the New Testament teaches about the unsaved. They are to be models of the grace of God in their lives and love David, even though he may remain unsaved and perish (see Rom. 9:28; Eph. 2:5).

Conclusion

The Lord can do what He wants with His creation (see Rom 9:21). Evangelism can start with prayer and may or may <u>not</u> happen. Evangelism can happen without prayer. It is the Lord that places a calling on someone's life to preach the gospel. This calling will <u>not</u> be in vain. Salvations will occur.

Some churches have a scheduled time of outreach or visitation. Occasionally, I have knocked on doors and seen results. One downside I noticed was that the participants believe that after outreach, they were done for the week. There is a lot of time and activity between church meetings. A strategy should be to train church members to use his or her time during the week, when they are out and about, in their particular harvest to influence the culture. This requires training during normal activities, like Jesus did with His disciples. For example, a church trainer can join a church member when they are out shopping. The results may involve Christian influence without salvation.

Pure religion and undefiled before God and the Father is this, to visit the fatherless and widows in their affliction, *and* to keep himself unspotted from the world. James 1:27

Jesus walked here and there, some places He needed to go to and other places He was asked to visit. Now, the church has been established by God to equip the saints for ministry (see Eph. 4:12). The question is, *"Has the church equipped the saints to minister in the public arena?"*

Chapter Nine

A Desire for Robots

Visionaries desire an ideal world (see Matt. 5:6). In an ideal world everyone would think, speak and live in harmony with God, family, neighbors and government. Everyone would eat the exact amount of food and work to keep the body at the perfect weight. This is possible. At least we should believe it to be.

> **Finally, brethren, whatsoever things are true, whatsoever things** *are* **honest, whatsoever things** *are* **just, whatsoever things** *are* **pure, whatsoever things** *are* **lovely, whatsoever things** *are* **of good report; if** *there be* **any virtue, and if** *there be* **any praise, think on these things.** Phil. 4:8

Charles Stanley states that, "*No one would like to be in a form physically, Spiritually and every other way in which you had no choices in life. You are just a robot. Everyday of your life this is how you operate.*"[1] Charles Stanley implies that no one would want that. The problem with choices is that man can make bad choices, and left alone by God, man will degenerate to where his choices are all bad, as in the day of Noah (see Gen. 6:5). Man has too many harmful choices, which appeal to the majority (see Matt. 7:13). Choices that appear to benefit self are later discovered to be a liability to self and others. The decision-making mind of man rarely chooses the way of life (see Matt. 7:14). I desire everyone to act like sons and daughters of God, obedient to a high level, similar to a robot.

I did <u>not</u> want to be a Christian. I was led to submit to a higher power. This is my personal testimony with the purpose of sharing an example of someone who did <u>not</u> choose Jesus as His Savior; instead was chosen to be one of His disciples (see John 15:16). I am <u>not</u> saying that I am an example of a robot of Jesus. Still, there were times when God intervened, perhaps for a few seconds that changed the direction of my life. There were situations that were out of my control and in His control. These were rare Spiritual robotics. Meanwhile, I discuss natural trials that I prefer to forget, but for the purpose of testimony I mention them here.

I was born in Augusta, Georgia to Victor "Mac" McCann and Mary "Edna" McCann. I have an older brother and an older sister. The youngest sibling, another brother, was born nine and a half years after me. My father had served in the army for eleven years and probably would have continued until retirement. After duty in World War II, I believe he felt more comfortable in civilian life with a family. My mother was a faithful member of a Southern Baptist church. I do <u>not</u> recall my father attending church and I do <u>not</u> know his Spiritual state. He died from a heart condition when I was thirteen.

Left to Right: John, his older sister and brother

Walls and Boundaries

My father said that I was such a good-looking boy that he hoped I would never grow up. He said I looked like Alan Ladd, the actor. That was fine except I struggled with two conditions that I can only explain as the providence of God. First, I had a severe over bite. When I was about nine years old, I was playing with a handmade cart on wheels. I would lie on my belly and ride down a concrete ramp from a storage shed that my father had made. It was like a surfboard on wheels. Somehow my head lunged down and my upper front teeth were chipped on the concrete. I often wondered how it happened! It was such a surprise to me. I now believe that it was an act of Holy Spirit that was preventing me from worldly ways (see Lam. 3:16). As I grew, I desperately wanted straight teeth. Once, I showed my teeth to my mother, but she just said something about Bugs Bunny. I assumed braces were too expensive on her limited income after my father's death. Secondly, I had poor eyesight. I was five and a half diopters nearsighted. In other words, I could not see distances. I was given eyeglasses in elementary school, but I did not wear them. Back then, boys wearing eyeglasses was difficult. If you could imagine a young boy sitting in class in just his underwear, that would be how I felt with eyeglasses. It was embarrassing to put the eyeglasses on around anyone, so I did not wear them. In fact, I did not even want to be near them. I can still remember the smell of the plastic frame and lens. These two conditions, the over bite and poor eyesight dramatically affected my life, perhaps preventing me from becoming a womanizing worldly intellect. Therefore, I am not a big free will advocate. For me it was like God took things away from me. This is difficult to explain, but He does something in your inward being whether by outward circumstances or inward tinkering or both. The below Scripture testifies to what God can do in the body, soul and Spirit of man.

> **Hath not the potter power over the clay, of the same lump to make one vessel unto honour, and another unto dishonour?** Rom. 9:21

First grade elementary school revealed that I was given a sensitive nature. My mother normally prepared our lunches before we left for school. One morning, she was late and said she would bring it to us. I do not know about my brother or sister; I think their class ate at a different time. I remember the anxiety as lunchtime was drawing near and my mother had not arrived. Finally, at lunchtime I felt like everyone's eyes were on me. Here I was sitting down with no lunch in front of me. A girl offered me part of her lunch, but the ordeal was too much. I walked over to the corner of the lunchroom and put my face to the wall and cried. No one could comfort me.

Another issue happened in first grade when this second grader would hit me in my nose. Due to this, my nose would start bleeding by itself. I do not remember how many times this second grader hit me. My mother said; if someone hits you, hit him back. Later, perhaps the fifth grade, a student sitting beside me at lunch placed something from his plate on mine. I took it and threw it back. We got into a bit of a wrestling match at the table. It was not much but it merited a paddling by the principle. Overall, being quite and passive seem to be my calling or nature due to my overbite and my poor vision.

My mother would regularly take us to church. This had both a positive and negative effect on me. I remember sitting in that church of about a hundred people and the Spirit of God moving about. I remember my mother giving me a quarter to put in the Sunday school offering. This was a great lesson at this young age for me to honor God. Negatively, there was a time when I was embarrassed and scolded unfairly from a young successful real estate man that taught Sunday school. I was about seven or eight, and he asked me to open the class in prayer. I said that I did not know how. This was unacceptable to him and he let me know. You might say I suffered a bit of damaged emotion for being honest. Another time during vacation Bible school, a boy said that the only reason I came was for the cookies and punch. Then, one day someone poured punch on my head from an upstairs rail and my hair got stiff after the punch dried. So I developed a dislike for church. I wrote a note stating that as an American I should be able to choose whether to attend church or not. I did not intend for my mother to read it, but somehow the note got into her hands. For some reason, she honored my request and I stayed home. Not attending church was a big mistake, but my conscience had been violated.

Due to my overbite, I developed a low self-esteem. I remember seeing people with straight teeth and pretty smiles.

I was envious. It seemed so distant for me. At sixteen, I went swimming at the lake with some friends. I remember coming out of the water and a skinny redheaded girl coming up and saying, "*come here*." Then she kissed me. This was probably common for most teenagers, but my teeth jammed into hers. For something that should have given pleasure, I was most embarrassed and intimidated. Later, I remember her laying on top of me in the back seat of the car. She was kissing me, but I pretended to be asleep. Except for her cigarette breath I may have conformed to the world of free love, but mostly because of my awful overbite. If I would have kissed her with my overbite she may have received a cut lip or tongue.

Even talking with my overbite was difficult. Many times when I talked, people would hold their hands over their mouth with a disturbed look on their face while viewing my awful overbite. This was traumatic for me. At the same time I would have these pretty girls look at me and want to talk, but I would freeze up. This is how life was for me. I had a desire to socialize and have fun, but faced embarrassment if I opened my mouth.

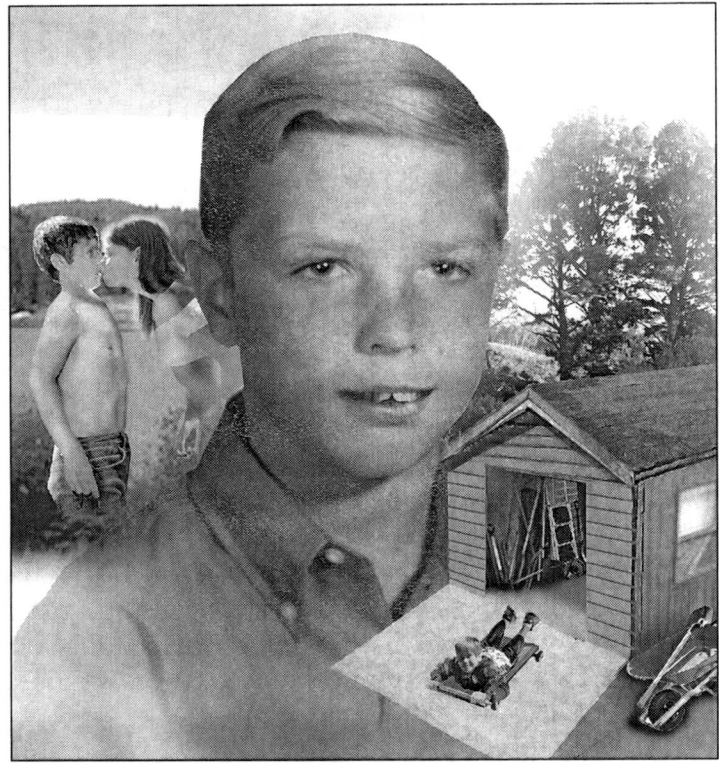

He hath also broken my teeth with gravel stones,
(Lam. 3:16)

My first automobile was a VW Sports Beetle. My sister had purchased the car with my mother co-signing. Then my sister's boyfriend drove it out to Orange County, California and sent her a plane ticket to meet him there. This left my mother to make the payments. After praying and tracing a phone call, my mother flew out to California and drove the car back. Then I took over the monthly payments after I starting working a part-time job. Things were falling in place for me. I was finishing a computer-programming course of study, had a job and now a car. I would soon have my teeth straightened with braces. My hope was that I would find a wonderful girl to marry and live happily ever after.

Closer to Home is the title of a Grand Funk song from the 1970's. I can identify with some of the lyrics while I was away from God and trying to do my own thing in this world.

> *I can feel the hand, of a stranger, And it's tightening, around my throat. Heaven help me, Heaven help me, Take this stranger from my boat.*

Fire Water

Drunk driving is a visual manifestation of serious issues within the culture. It is an act of the flesh (see Gal. 5:21). In my early twenties, I would drink and drive, but after two or three DUI arrests, I would take a taxi, walk, bicycle or hitch hike. If prohibition of alcohol had been successful in the United States, I would have benefited. Since alcohol was legal and people around me were drinking, I thought it was acceptable. Alcohol was my helpmate toward a downward spiral. Except for the interventions of God I would have been another victim of early death from foolish choices. Alcohol was a personality changer for me. I could come home from work on Friday afternoon feeling very tired and within an hour be changed. I would start with beer before transitioning to bourbon whiskey or scotch. Then I would go out and order drinks. A typical evening would end after the bars closed. I might go to a Waffle House for food and then go home and drink some more while listening to music until I was too tired to stay awake. The evening may have involved playing pool, singing with the jukebox or band or an occasional dance. I remember one evening in particular when I slow danced, held and kissed a young lady while the band was playing in a South Augusta club. I remember how wonderful that was. (*In my early twenties I had braces on my teeth.*) She was wearing some type of sparkling makeup on her cheeks and some rubbed off on my face. However, I did not leave the club with her. Alcohol made me wander. I might visit three or more clubs each night.

Weapon of Choice

When a disturbance happens once, you might ignore it as part of life. When the same disturbance happens again and again, you realize that something is wrong and the disturbance has your attention. Let's say lighting strikes the tree in front of your house one day. You settle with the insurance company and you are glad no one was hurt. Then three weeks later you are visiting uncle Bob in another state and lighting strikes the tree in front of uncle Bob's house. Again lighting strikes while you are visiting friends in your neighborhood. You start to wonder like Job after he lost his possessions, children, health and peace of mind (see Job 1:13-19, 2:7). However, Job's many disturbances were rapid occurrences and different from each other. My single disturbance repeated over gaps of time like a repeated strike of destructive lighting. And Job was left with something I never had, a wife. Yet disturbances appear necessary.

Before I was saved, I can remember what it was like to have a conscience of right and wrong. I believed there was a God from my Christian upbringing but I had no desire to know Him or sit in church. I wanted to do my own thing and would have if things had gone my way. However, God controls and directs. He can arrange and rearrange the furniture on the stage of the world to accomplish His will. I did _not_ like that, but I learned I could _not_ resist Him.

I might have been better in a culture where parents arrange the selection of a spouse. As much as I love America, I did _not_ fit well in the social realm and especially in the culture around me. "*What do you think of Jeanie?*" a friend asked me. "*You can't be shy around her, because she's _not_,*" the friend added. Here I was this young eighteen-year-old man, raised in church, traumatized at sixteen with my first kiss and now expected to be this free love Romeo. The girls did _not_ like my hesitations. They had immediate demands. Before I could get to know someone and calm my dental woes, I was targeted for destruction by a disappointed female weapon thrower. The weapon of choice was free love by trying to make me jealous with any male friend around me. Now I am <u>not</u> a polished movie actor or a wealthy good-looking musician, so my best guess for what happened was beyond me. I needed to call out to God for help, and I think this is what God wanted. At times the situation would go to absurdity. I was <u>not</u> just a by-stander, but was looked upon as the cause. *"He's got to find a way to keep us critters out of his throne room,"* said one co-worker. Another compared my traumatic emotional experience with his in Vietnam. Another cynically said, *"It's a great world, isn't it, John?"* Another liked having me around to provide opportunities with the women. In my carnal nature, I preferred to join them at the *"beauty shop,"* the reference to one young woman's house they visited at lunch.

> **As a jewel of gold in a swine's snout,** *so is* **a fair woman which is without discretion.**
> Prov. 11:22

Please. I hope I do <u>not</u> sound like I am suffering from delusions of grandeur, as one Christian counselor implied. He thought I was this guy who daydreamed about these beautiful women that were in love with me. No, instead I am trying to be as realistic and honest as I can with words. I preferred none of these occurrences. Once, I considered stepping up and talking to one of my female troublemakers. I sought the advice of a pastor. He counseled me, *"Stay away from her. She's trouble."*

History reveals the power of a beautiful woman over a man, while Scripture states that one can be delivered (see Prov. 2:16). I could speculate that these women would have acted ungodly without me being there, but <u>not</u> to the level that it reached. At times, I would notice that their conscience would bother them about these acts. Still, within a group, they continued on, like robots of the flesh.

Although I prefer to forget, I can name several women where this similar event occurred over gaps of time. This may be common in a troubled marriage or this may be common all across America. People love an excuse that satisfies his or her conscience toward living a life of lust. My prayer and thoughts were that they would find the right guy to marry. Yet I was cautiously pessimistic that I was the guy. These actions, whatever the motive, were shutting the door of my heart. Instead of liberty, it is often bondage women find. I believe these women wanted a husband, but on their terms. Yet they were bound by the works of the flesh and acted accordingly. That is why I am <u>not</u> a strong free will advocate. I see the will of people bound to their nature, whether carnal or Spiritual. Jesus compares humans to crops and trees that bring forth fruit according to their nature (see Matt. 7:17-19). I have observed this principle. I have experienced times when everyone did what was right in his or her own eyes and God appears to have given them over to their own lustful nature (see Rom. 1:24). At this time in my life, I did <u>not</u> have a strong Spiritual person around me since I had left church. In fact, some of the participants were church members. In my struggle between good and evil, evil was winning. These events damaged by soul (see II Pet. 2:8). Consider the following fictional anecdote.

> An attractive young lady lived in a small town with only one pharmacy. The married pharmacist flirted with the young lady and desired her. When she refused, the pharmacist would delay her prescriptions. Then she moved to an apartment in the city. The apartment manager asked for a date, but she refused. She later became suspicious when her maintenance requests for repairs were delayed for long periods.

Only One Way

My past woes had blinded me to believe I could find a nice lady to marry. I may have been all right if I could just go to work and be left alone to do my job. <u>Not</u> so. Along would come this beautiful tiger woman, far beyond my league, that would put her claws in me by enticing my co-workers. I had no shield of faith to quench the fiery darts of the enemy (see Eph. 6:16). My refuge was alcohol, which helped me escape temporarily. I was disgusted with the way people acted and I did not know how to change things. The prophet Jeremiah experienced this.

> **Oh that I had in the wilderness a lodging place of wayfaring men; that I might leave my people, and go from them! for they** *be* **all adulterers, an assembly of treacherous men.** Jer. 9:2

I would not consciously end my life, but I would drink and put others and myself in harm's way. By the grace of God I never hurt anyone from my two automobile accidents. Both cars rolled over several times and were total losses. One of my co-workers said that I had a death wish. When it seemed that I could not even die, I saw only one way forward.

My weakness to rely on alcohol for comfort from the licentious environment I worked around led me to stay out of work drunk. I was asked to resign when I returned to work and I did resign. I called my mother and said that I would see her in church on Wednesday night. At the age of twenty-nine I returned to church. I would like to believe that I made this choice to return to church and that I deserve some credit. It would not have happened left to myself. When I say, "returned to church," I mean that God was dealing with my nature. When I entered church that night, I experienced the Spirit of God and I knew I was finally heading in the right direction.

A Glint of Heaven

In 1986, I attended a cell group sponsored by a young Presbyterian doctor. Denominations are interesting. I have heard Presbyterians described as "*snobs*" and "*proud*". Please these are not my words. I would say the average Presbyterian has a college degree with all the social graces, which is fine. However, I felt a bit uncomfortable during the cell group introduction when everyone was asked to describe themselves. They usually started with the college they graduated from and some fine colleges were mentioned. I was the only one in the group of about ten men without a college degree. I preferred to share my salvation experience, but I assume most were raised in church and it was a similar experience. Nevertheless, I continued coming. The group usually ended about 8:30 PM. One night while driving home I had a most wonderful experience. For a second or two, I saw a vision (see Acts 2:17; Eph. 1:17-18). The vision did not reveal a lot of color or image. It was just a sky like image that I understood to be the entrance or dome of a wonderful place, perhaps heaven. The best part was the way it made me feel, although feeling is not the best explanation. It was a complete feeling of what I was to become and I must say that I liked it. I was closer to home. It was a real experience that connected with me so much that I was able to stop drinking alcohol or better stated, "The Lord took the alcohol away." Afterward, the cigarettes departed. I remember going into work one morning and announcing to my co-workers that I had quit smoking. They asked when my last cigarette was and I said about 9:00 PM last night. Someone cynically said, "*sure,*" but the cigarettes were gone for me.

Labor of Learning

During a group lunch with friends in the computer field, a young lady said that she was taking some Bible courses. That struck a chord with me. That is what I needed since I had left church for fifteen years and I was not familiar with the Bible. So I started taking courses from a small school in South Augusta affiliated with a non-denominational church. Next I went two years to a Bible College for preachers. Later, I joined the church that sponsored the college from encouragement by the students. This was not God's plan for me in joining that church. I also joined the choir and was placed beside an attractive young woman. I liked her, but the old demons came out. She discovered where I worked and started seeing one of my co-workers and another employee. This troubled me. Once at the prayer altar, the Spirit took control of my prayer of distress and out came a language that many heard including the pastor. He ceased the prayers by switching to a song. The pastor later told me the altar was a Baptist altar. Soon I realized that I was not going to continue as a member when the pastor sided with the attractive young woman. Her family were long time members. I believe his words from the pulpit were, *"the women of this church will knock you out."* Finally, I encountered resistance when registering for my third year of Bible College (primarily due to another event at the Baptist altar) and I realized I was not welcomed. I wrote the pastor and he wrote me a nice letter back and we left it at that. That church was not perfect, but I would recommend it. I learned that I did not have the free will to join the church of my choice. My doctrine was right, but my application was wrong. You do not go into another denomination and taunt their beliefs: unless God has sent you.

In the fall of 1991, Erskine Theological Seminary brought classes to University Hospital (where I was born) and I took three courses. Due to time restraints I could not continue with Erskine, but instead took some correspondent courses from Moody Bible Institution and Columbia Bible College. For a short time, Lee College offered two or three courses at a local church. Most of my studies have been with Christian Life School of Theology (CLST). CLST is established by God, but not accredited by man. CLST offers a short cut to a doctrinal degree. Man establishes heavy means to an accredited degree, like trying to drink water from a fire hydrant. I love Scripture and I am a bit laden with the labor in this life, but I come to Jesus and learn of Him (Bible school). It is easy.

Come unto me, all *ye* that labour and are heavy laden, and I will give you rest. Take my yoke upon you, and learn of me; for I am meek and lowly in heart: and *ye* shall find rest unto your souls. For my yoke *is* easy, and my burden is light. Matt. 11:28-30

An Ivory Sculpture

One afternoon in 1992 while I was studying in my small rented house in North Augusta, South Carolina, the Lord spoke in my innermost being. It was not audible, but I understood the message, *"Don't ever hurt her."* A feeling came over me that made a big impression. It was not a passive feeling like we normally experience in reaction to an event in life, but an active feeling placed there by God. God understands emotions, because he placed an emotional reaction within me. If you can image a little child that loves his father and accidentally did something wrong and was disciplined, this is how I felt. Yet I had not done anything. It was a message not to ever hurt her or I was going to greatly disappoint my Heavenly Father. However, who was "her"? I discussed this with some of my friends at Erskine Theological Seminary. One said, *"Oh John, I see a beautiful woman like an ivory sculpture. She is fragile so be careful."* Another said, *"I believe the Lord is going to send you a wife that has been hurt in the past and you are to heal her."* These sounded good, but both were wrong.

The Lord uses a father and a mother to bring new physical life into the world. When someone does not honor his or her father and mother, they are insulting the means that God used to bring them life (see Exod. 20:12). It became apparent to me that the Lord wanted me to help my mother. I know the Lord is not a respecter of persons, but I think about my mother, a petite 5' 2" Southern Baptist lady with a meek and sweet personality that the Lord thought enough of to seriously warn me about neglecting (see I Tim. 5:8). So I helped my mother. Later, she broke her wrist and I started driving her to church.

Once a courtesy office at my apartment building stopped his police car as my mother and I were walking to my apartment. He had a surprised look on his face and said, *"John, the Lord had me stop and tell you that He is going to bless you for taking care of your mother."* I knew it was genuine by the look on his face. He kept making the point that the Lord had him stop; it was <u>not</u> his idea. That encouraged me. Eventually I had to take my mother to church in a wheelchair. Later, I hired another caregiver while I was at work. My mother passed away August 31, 2003 at 1:47 PM. She was seventy-nine. The Lord was gracious to let me know that this was her time.

A few months later I fell asleep on my couch one evening. I would have been late for work except the Lord woke me with the words, *"No school today?"* What did these words mean? I concluded that He wanted me to continue studying, so I started back with Christian Life School of Theology. I have heard many words from earth with little or no change in my life. Meanwhile, only a few words from heaven have made dramatic change. Realizing His awareness, I prayed for ten additional years since I had <u>not</u> experienced a good social life. Surprisingly, the Lord replied *"twenty years"*.

I can only imagine what my life would have been like with straight teeth and good vision in my early years. I could be a hundred pounds over weight with beer in the refrigerator, divorced three times, with a shabby beard. I could have excelled in academics, becoming very liberal and worldly and viewing Christianity as an antiquated religion for the narrowed minded. I can only imagine what my life would have been like if God had <u>not</u> intervened. Due to my weakness with alcohol, I could have landed a prison sentence for automobile manslaughter. I could have died in one of the wrecks. My choices could have brought about any one of these, but God placed boundaries, which prevented them.

> **thou hast appointed his bounds that he cannot pass;** Job 14:5b

My theological views were influenced from experiences. I am <u>not</u> a fatalist believing that man has no power to change the future and is destined to a fixed fate. I believe man has the power to act according to his nature. I have seen married men that have vowed to be faithful to their wives, yet unable to resist when given the opportunity to have a beautiful woman. They act according to their nature. Still, I do <u>not</u> see man always operating independent of God's influence. I cannot explain how on two separate nights, my car crashed and rolled over several times and I survived. God does intervene. The concept of God allowing evil is vague and best left unanswered as far as developing an academic doctrine. We know that Satan comes to steal, kill and destroy through deception, lies and temptations. Satan would dominate every carnal man except for man's conscience to judge right and wrong. God would robotically lead a Spiritual man except for man's competing carnal nature. These operations are vague to man. If man could understand and control these dynamics, he could solve the problems of the world.

> **For the grace of God that bringeth salvation hath appeared to all men, Teaching us that, denying ungodliness and worldly lusts, we should live soberly, righteously, and godly, in this present world; Looking for that blessed hope, and the glorious appearing of the great God and our Saviour Jesus Christ; Who gave himself for us, that he might redeem us from all iniquity, and purify unto himself a peculiar people, zealous of good works.** Titus 2:11-14

Christians do <u>not</u> fit in this present world. This present world is laced with lies and disobedience (see Eph. 2:2). A normal Christian life is operating with persecution and misunderstanding. A shield of faith is needed to look beyond. When you have a glimpse of what is ahead, the present is bearable (see Rom. 8:18). The Word is true and through the ministry of

Holy Spirit, Christians can grow in the grace and knowledge of the Lord Jesus Christ.

Thankfully and mercifully, free will did <u>not</u> prevail in my life. Now, my desire is for everyone to operate similar to robots of Jesus.

> **Blessed** *are* **they which do hunger and thirst after righteousness: for they shall be filled.** Matt. 5:6

Chapter Ten

Natural Robots

Nature is the physical world and the processes that control the physical world. Without revelation from the Creator, natural man can only observe the physical world (see Deut. 4:19). This is called science. From science, man reasons and establishes theories. Theories are <u>not</u> science. Natural man falsely theorizes that the natural processes are constant and stable, that all things continue as they always have. This is called uniformitarianism (see II Pet. 3:4). Next, natural man assumes you can reverse the order to calculate the age of the earth and universe. Natural man is ignorant of the global flood that rapidly created phenomena like the Grand Canyon (see Gen. 7; II Pet. 3:6). Instead natural man predicts sites like the Grand Canyon took many years to fashion and they presumptuously calculate large ages of time. However, the global flood was catastrophic, so much so, that the former world perished and now we have another world (see II Pet. 3:5-7).

Without revelation, natural man attempts to determine the different rankings of life. The FARM acrostic is used as a scale of progression: fish, amphibians, reptiles to mammals. Within mammals, monkeys progressed into men. This is called evolution. Evolution is a natural conclusion from natural reasoning. With the revelation from the Creator, the picture is different. The rankings are fixed (see Gen. 1:12, 21, 24, 25).

Man has access to many natural elements. He can drill for oil, harvest food, raise livestock and build structures. However, man is passive toward many natural elements, such as the wind. Likewise, man is passive toward the distribution of the gifts of the Spirit, including faith and salvation (see John 3:8). Finding a man preaching the Word of faith does **not** put the control with man (see Rom. 10:15). You can think that man controls the distribution of faith, but you cannot support man's control of faith from Scripture (see I Cor. 12:11). A gap exists between the access and control of the natural elements and the control of the Spiritual. God controls the Spiritual because God is Spirit. Even though natural man can access natural elements, he controls little. If man had the faith the size of a grain of mustard seed or the faith that God has, he could say unto a mountain "**be removed and be cast into the sea**" (see Matt. 17:20; I Cor. 13:2b). Still, man can do a little. With cloud seeding, man attempts to increase rain and snow activity (see Job 38:34). Microevolution is selective breeding within types. This is possible for man to do with animals, but God has fixed natural boundaries that man cannot change. Man can also tweak seed production. Wheat, for example, has changed dramatically in the past fifty years under the influence of agricultural scientists.[1] This has been profitable for the producers, but detrimental for the health of the consumers. However, ultimately, the Creator has fixed the large picture of nature.

Mother nature is an analogy of the harmony of the natural world. The role of a mother is to produce and nurture life. When nature is in harmony it is credited to mother nature, but when natural disaster occurs it is an act of God. I disagree with the mother nature analogy. I prefer a robot analogy. The sun sets and rises and robotically advances to the next day. The animals are programmed (instinctively) to survive in an environment of trees, plants and prey. Many bits of life and activity survive without any help or disturbance from man (see Job 38:35-41). When a natural disaster occurs, I prefer the advice of Jesus, **not** to blame the victims' lifestyles, but for everyone to examine his or her own life. "**Nay: but, except ye repent, ye shall all likewise perish**" (Luke 13:3).

Just how much Satan controls or is allowed to control is unknown to man. Before the fall, Satan spoke through the serpent to Eve in the garden (see Gen. 3:1; Rev. 12:9). Therefore Satan controlled the serpent since the tongue is the most untamable member (see Jam. 3:8). Some speculate that all animals possessed understandable language before the fall since Eve was <u>not</u> startled by the words from the serpent.

Before the flood of Noah, the environment was substantially better than today. Just to breath the air was a pleasure. This was a good place to live (see Gen 1:31). Man, animals and plants lived longer and more abundantly. Reptiles, unlike other mammals, continue to grow in size and due to their extended lifecycles became the dinosaur fossils discovered after the flood of Noah. Dinosaurs are referred to as dragons and behemoths (see Job 30:29, 40:15).[2] Scripture states that dinosaurs and man lived together. However, evolutionists will strongly disagree, even within a cartoon like the Flintstones. In fact, there are expensive structures with highly paid staff members, teaching well-written manuscripts with vivid illustrations that disagree, but Truth is <u>not</u> always found in the wisdom, glamour and wealth of this natural world. Ultimately, it is <u>not</u> the role of the Spiritual man to reconstruct the flesh and manners of dinosaurs in order to win a debate with natural man. Dinosaurs became extinct due to the change of oxygen and food supply after the flood of Noah.

> **And God said, Let there be a firmament in the midst of the waters, and let it divide the waters from the waters. And God made the firmament and divided the waters which** *were* **under the firmament from the waters which** *were* **above the firmament, and it was so.** Gen 1:6-7

It is <u>not</u> a stretch from Scripture to place a vapor canopy above the near atmosphere that kept the oxygen content richer with less radiation from the sun, which slowed down the aging process (see Gen. 7:11; II Pet. 3:5). Much of the water on the surface today was in a canopy above. I envision the sky to be the color of a rainbow due to the prism from the sun.³ The rainbow sky was a window of heaven (see Gen 7:11b). This created a beautiful multicolored atmosphere to gaze upon which was similar to the rainbow round about the throne in heaven (see Ezek. 1:28; Rev. 4:3).

The Creator judges and changes His creation as He sees fit. The ground was cursed when Adam and Eve sinned while the sky was cursed in the catastrophic judgment of the flood of Noah.

> **cursed is the ground for thy sake; in sorrow shalt thou eat of it all the days of thy life;** Gen 3:17b

> **and the windows of heaven were opened.** Gen 7:11b

A local event was the destruction of Sodom and Gomorra and the parting of the Red Sea (see Gen. 19:24; Exod. 14:21). Later, Jesus calmed the wind and sea (see Matt. 8:26).

Plants and Trees

Before the flood of Noah the primary role of plants and the fruit from trees was food for man and animals (see Gen. 1:29-30). The uniform surface of the earth without mountains, oceans, ice caps or deserts allowed growth and abundance. The great food and oxygen supply before the flood sustained life longer.

Take a moment and look at a tree. Ask yourself, "*What did I have to do with the making of this tree?*" I think of a poem I learned in elementary school. I still remember the side of the board where Miss Hayes wrote.

Trees by Joyce Kilmer 1886–1918

I THINK that I shall never see
A poem lovely as a tree.

A tree whose hungry mouth is prest
Against the sweet earth's flowing breast;

> A tree that looks at God all day,
> And lifts her leafy arms to pray;
>
> A tree that may in summer wear
> A nest of robins in her hair;
>
> Upon whose bosom snow has lain;
> Who intimately lives with rain.
>
> Poems are made by fools like me,
> But only God can make a tree.

In today's public school system, this poem's reference to God would be shunned. Christians in earlier generations in America overreached within the public school system using shame and even harassment that backfired on their sincere efforts to evangelize.

Moving Creatures

After the flood of Noah, the primary role of all moving creatures was food for man (see Gen. 9:3). Creatures move to and fro until they are prepared and placed in the mouths of men and women. In judgment, the Creator can reverse this (see Ezek. 39:17-20).

What modern science calls instinct or innate behavior is how the Creator has programmed moving creatures to behave in a certain manner without prior experience or learning (see Job 39). The diet of moving creatures is determined by their design from creation. A giraffe will <u>not</u> eat a dead wildebeest and a lion will <u>not</u> eat tree leaves. That is why a Christian has a desire for the Word of God while a natural person desires the things of the world. His or her nature is different (see I Cor. 2:14).

Animals have souls and make decisions. Scholars are timid to relate souls to animals, but they do <u>not</u> deny it is in the language of the Bible.[4] The Hebrew word "*nephesh*" is translated "**soul**" when it applies to man, but is suspiciously translated "**life**" when it applies to animals (see Lev. 17:11-14). Animals with souls cast a shadow on soul winning and the immortality of the soul. Yet Jesus called Herod, "**that fox**," which reveals how Herod made decisions similar to the soul of a fox (see Luke 13:31-32). Obedience training for animals is similar to man learning to obey the laws of right living (see Prov. 26:11). For an animal, such as a dog to go through obedience training is a lower form of soul winning toward man (see Prov. 11:30; Matt. 7:6a). Therefore soul winning is training in obedient living on earth, not birth into the Kingdom.

Scripture reveals how the Creator is able to modify the souls of animals. After the flood of Noah the fear of man was placed within the soul of animals and they virtually avoid man (see Gen. 9:2). When they do attack, the fear is still there. The fear of man was necessary because the Creator changed the diet of certain animals to include flesh.

How the Creator controls each moving creature on a 24 hour/7 day basis is unknown by man. Nevertheless, Scripture has examples of this control. The Lord opened the mouth of a donkey and the donkey spoke (see Num. 22:28). Ravens fed Elijah (see I Kings 17:4). Jonah was trapped in the belly of a great fish for three days (see Jonah 1:17). Jesus said there is not a sparrow that falls to the ground without the Father's permission (see Matt. 10:29). The fish obeyed Jesus when He asked the disciples to cast their nets on the other side of the boat. Their nets became full of fish (see John 21:6).

Universe

The creation of the universe is described in one (uni) verse:

In the beginning God created the heaven and the earth. Gen. 1:1

Would man build a robot that he could not control? Has God created a universe that He cannot control? The universe is like one gigantic robot that God created and set in motion. He commands it as He sees fit.

Illustrations

Scripture uses illustrations from the natural world:

- In the covenants between God and man,
- The words of the Old Testament prophetic language,
- And the teaching of Jesus to describe the Kingdom of God.

Jesus admitted that the natural world could not completely illustrate the Kingdom due to man's limited exposure to Kingdom truths (see Luke 13:18). Still, these illustrations are the best teaching tools since the natural world dimly mirrors the Spiritual world.

Conclusion

The natural world declares the glory of God and provides food, shelter and clothing for man. Nature is the theater in which His power and majesty is showcased.[5] God has fixed the boundaries of the natural world. Man can micro manage the natural world within these boundaries. Likewise, man can micromanage his daily activities, but God has fixed the boundaries of nature and world events.

Just as God can control nature, God can control man. Like a robot of Jesus, man writes Scripture, speaks in different languages, builds an ark and travels the land to evangelize. These acts glorify the Creator's ability to control man (see Rom. 4:2, 20).

Man is a hopeless case without the control of God. The first earth was destroyed because God was sorry He had made man, not because He had made the animals, plants and universe. The natural world obeys God while natural man rebels (see Nahum 1:3-5). However, the end of the world is near (see Matt. 24:3).

As time moves forward, food spoils, wood rots and people age. This is the decaying process called entropy. Entropy is a law where things go into disorder and time must be present for change or disorder to occur. But time is a temporary commodity in this current natural world. There is an expiration date on the current earth and some big changes are coming.

The below events are described in Scripture, although scholars disagree when the rapture, tribulations, judgments, etc. will occur. The Lord does what He wants whenever He wills, even raising folks from their graves before the rapture (see Matt. 27:53).

- Church age (present)
- Rapture
- Seven year of tribulations
- Salvation of Jews
- Battle at Armageddon
- Satan bound
- Millennial
- Final battle of Satan at beloved city: Jerusalem (Rev. 20:7-9)
- Last Day: Judgment of individuals
- End of age (time no longer)

that there should be time no longer: Rev. 10:6b

One final stage on earth will include a temple in Jerusalem during the **millennial** (see Ezek. 40-48). The Lord will reign and Israel and other nations will worship as intended in the old covenant (see Isa. 2:1-5). Even though Israel was given all the natural resources in the old covenant, the Spirit was needed to fulfill the will of God in worship (see Isa. 11). This reign will transpire for a thousand years or a millennial. God will make sure that worship is done properly, <u>not</u> by force, but by His Spirit (see Zech. 4:6, 14:16).

No one knows the time of the end, <u>not</u> even the Son because the Father has <u>not</u> set a time (see Mark 13:32). As soon as the Father sets the time, the Son will know. Afterwards, there will be a new heaven and a new earth where righteousness dwells. The elements will be burned with fire. Whether the new heaven and the new earth are created anew or become a transfiguration of the former, it will be a place prepared by God for His people (see II Pet. 3:10-13; Rev. 21).

The natural process of entropy will disappear along with the realm of time. Arriving late cannot happen in the heavenly. Food will <u>not</u> spoil. Hair will <u>not</u> turn grey. There will <u>not</u> be any manmade creations and designs. No automobiles, houses, clothing, robots or anything that man makes. The old things will pass away.

> **In my Father's house are many mansions: if it were not so, I would have told you. I go to prepare a place for you.** John 14:2

Everything and everybody will live and act in harmony with God. The children of God will be filled which hungered and thirsted after righteousness (see Matt. 5:6). A sinless realm will be fixed similar to a top-of-the-line robot.

Chapter Eleven

Auxiliary Parts

This is the chapter where I placed auxiliary parts or subjects that support the robotic theme. Each part has a subject heading. One subject "Willful Sin" was moved here from Chapter 1.

Wordsmith

A wordsmith is a writer or speaker who uses a toolbox of words to construct a document or speech. The below lists are words I avoid and words I use.

I Avoid These Words

- <u>Balance</u>: This word can be used to compromise truth by assuming a middle ground should exist to be fair. You might infer that being balanced is neither hot nor cold, but lukewarm (see Rev. 3:16).

- <u>Clearly</u>: I find this adverb is often used to strength the writer/speaker's assumptions. I am suspicious when I encounter this adverb.

- <u>Luck</u>: Luck is the cousin of chance and implies beyond any control. Luck is an abstract concept that ignores skill.[1] The popular "good luck" exhortation should be "God bless" (see Ruth 2:4).

- Must: This word is seldom found in the New Testament, except in the fulfillment of prophecy or a call on someone's life.

- No Problem: I am suspicious when people say "no problem." From my experience, they use it to make you feel good, but later I discovered it was a false claim.

- Shock: The meaning of this word has weakened because of over-usage. It appears to be just an exaggeration to draw attention.

- Spilled: I avoid using the verb "spilled" in relationship to the Blood of Christ. Spilled implies an accident in which the substance was wasted. The Blood of Christ was shed, not spilled.

- Surrender: This word is popular in free will Christian circles, but lacks a doctrinal basis in New Testament thought.

- Unfortunately/Fortunately: These words are very popular, but they have a secular anti-Christian origin (see Isa. 65:11).

I Use These Words

- Most: I use this word sparingly. I question the accuracy of statements where "*most*" is used. For example, "*Most Christians don't have a clue what the Bible says.*" Perhaps these statements come from surveys, but I question surveys that give statistics of opinions.

- Perhaps: I believe we do see some things dimly, so I use "perhaps" as a way to show the direction I lean (see I Cor. 13:12).

- Religion: I use this word sparingly because it is found in solid Christian documents. Those who say, "*I'm not religious, I have a relationship with Jesus,*" sound like they are boastfully proclaiming they are religious.

Interpretation

Correct interpretation involves reading meaning out of Scripture (exegesis) into the human mind. This is the same direct of flow in salvation; faith comes into the heart of man, not man placing his faith in God. The opposite of reading meaning out of Scripture is reading meaning into Scripture (eisegesis). One should exercise discipline not to read meaning into Scripture, nor to read between the lines. An example of reading meaning into Scripture is stating, "*We know that Judas Iscariot was once a Christian.*" Another example of reading meaning into Scripture is, "*The Bible tells us that God has given us free will.*" The correct answer may be, "*I don't know.*" Reading meaning into Scripture can create a stronghold, a place where one can hang his or her academic hat. So it is with free will. A private interpretation of **"whosoever shall"** becomes the foundation of salvation based upon the free will of man (see Rom. 10:17). Does the Bible tell us that God has given us free will? While the term "*free will*" never appears in the Scriptures in a technical, philosophical or theological sense, it is fair to say that in different ways the Bible both affirms and denies that people have free will.[2] To be specific, the Bible affirms that people have limited free will only in the natural world (see Gen. 3:6; Luke 12:4).

In interpretation, scholars have theological biases, which are found in the dictionaries, journals, study Bibles and other writings. There is much to consider in interpretation in order to rightly divide the Word. Your definition should include all of Scripture (see Luke 4:4). A common shortcoming is to see one occurrence, such as "**whosoever shall**" and establish and settle your definition while ignoring the whole of Scripture. "**Whosoever**" is better interpreted to imply that there is no difference between the Jew and the Gentile concerning salvation (see Rom. 10:12-13). Another Scripture, II Peter 3:9 is privately interpreted to imply that it is God's will that everyone be saved and therefore the choice is solely by man, not God (cf. John 1:13).

> **The Lord is not slack concerning His promise, as some count slackness, but is longsuffering <u>toward us</u>, not willing that <u>any</u> should perish but that <u>all</u> should come to repentance. II Pet. 3:9**

In context, the Scripture above links repentance with a sustained culture, not Spiritual salvation. Repentance keeps the culture from perishing, just as a lack of repentance in Noah's day led to the global flood where the people perished (see II Pet. 3:6). Repentance is something that man can do. Salvation is something only God can do. Repentance is one of the works that prove saving faith (see Jam. 2:20). Therefore, God is righteous to judge both the saved and the unsaved, because they have the ability to change their mind, which affects their behavior. This is the area of responsibility. However, this does not deny there are times when the Spirit of God can control an individual to perform robotic acts that are controlled by God (see Gen. 6:22; Acts 2:4). Still, the global flood destroyed the unrepentant. They perished.

The book of II Peter was written to the Elect (see II Pet. 1:2) and therefore the phrase, "**toward us**" (see underline above) narrows the scope to the Elect. The promise of His coming is toward the Elect (see II Pet. 3:4). It is God's will that all of His elect repent. If it were God's will that all be saved, all would be saved. Nevertheless, there is heavenly counsel unknown to man (see Deut. 29:29). His desire is for all to repent and save their culture, but not His will for all to enter His kingdom (see I Tim. 2:4). You may desire another house, car, etc., but you do not always use your will to "make it happen" (see Exod. 32:10-14).

Choice

It is easy to say that you make your own choices using free will, but what are your choices based upon? Choices cannot be sometimes new and independent within you. Instead your choices are a result of your nature, which agrees with the principles established by the Lord God or the god of this world. Saying that you make your own choices using free will is a result of the darkness established by someone else. Scripture testifies to a range of words and deeds: that of a fool and that of a wise man.

> **The fool hath said in his heart,** *There is* **no God.** Ps. 14:1a

> **Therefore whosoever heareth these sayings of mine, and doeth them, I will liken him unto a wise man, which built his house upon a rock:** Matt. 7:24

You cannot do whatever you want in society because of laws. You cannot do whatever you want in the moral realm because of your conscience and spiritual principles. You can disobey the laws, your conscience and spiritual principles, if this is your definition of free will. However, you are acting out of ignorance, rebellion or deception. God in His wisdom has allowed man to believe that he has free will, but man in his wisdom realizes that he does not have free will (see Prov. 1:29-33).

> **Thus saith the LORD, Let not the wise** *man* **glory in his wisdom, neither let the mighty** *man* **glory in his might, let not the** *rich* **man**

> **glory in his riches: But let him that glorieth glory in this, that he understandeth and knoweth me, that I *am* the LORD which exercise lovingkindness, judgment, and righteousness, in the earth: for in these** *things* **I delight, saith the LORD.** Jer. 9:23-24

Sin

Sin is missing the mark. The mark is the glory of acting like God, Who cannot sin (see Rom. 3:23). Sin has a desire to rule your life and sin receives power and strength from the law of God (see Gen. 4:7; Rom. 7:20; I Cor. 15:56). To be obedient, you must be plugged into another Source, just like a robot is plugged into a command center made by man. Sin is a malfunction. Someone has to pay for the malfunction for justice to prevail (see Col. 2:14). The Lord has an amazing visual and audio recording of all the words and deeds from the beginning to the end and will not leave one word or one deed unaccounted for. Sin is not removed after you forget about it. You do not go to sleep and wake up sinless. A lie must be paid for, like unpaid taxes. Time does not dissolve the sin. Sins are stored up until judgment (see Rom. 2:5). These may be coded on the soul. The Blood of Jesus can wash away the sins of the soul, including purging the conscience from harmful memories (see Heb. 9:14). The idea that "I can forgive, but not forget," may be just a myth (see Phil. 3:13).

Willful Sin

Caution: Due to the mature content, this subject was moved from chapter 1 in hopes that the reader would not be prematurely shaken by the solemn exhortation (see John 16:4b).

Christian advocates of free will appeal to the principle that every sin has been forgiven, past, present and future. Scripture states that many sins were forgiven and that many sins are being forgiven by the precious Blood of Jesus, but not every sin (see Matt. 26:28; Heb. 9:28). Consider willful sin.

> **For if we sin wilfully after that we have received the knowledge of the truth, there remaineth no more sacrifice for sins,** Heb. 10:26

Scripture has corrected me concerning the payment of sin. I have traditionally been taught that the cross paid for all sins. However, additional study has corrected my traditional belief.

I will clarify to avoid misunderstandings.

- The Blood of Jesus paid for sin and is the only means to inherit eternal life. The grace of God is vast but not without wisdom against disobedience.
- Forgiveness is available for sin after salvation.
- Forgiveness is not the only method of payment for sin.
- Payment for willful sin by the Christian is through judgment and suffering without loss of Spiritual salvation.
- By sufferings the punishment due for sin is cancelled.[3]
- By suffering for willful sin, the Christian understands the sufferings of Christ and learns obedience.
- Christians may suffer innocently and be rewarded.
- Payment for sins by the unbeliever is through judgment and suffering until the price has satisfied the justice of God.
- The unbeliever will perish once the price has been paid.

Just as Jesus took up the cross to suffer for our redemption, we must take up our cross to suffer for our willful sin of disobedience. For rewards in heaven, we suffer persecution (see Luke 9:22-24; Matt. 5:10-12). Only the one-time suffering by Jesus completed our Spiritual salvation, but two additional types of suffering complete our sanctification.

- **The cross for salvation/redemption**

- Willful sin for disobedience
- Reward for persecution

Tradition states that Jesus paid it all. Tradition is eager to find a favorable solution and a popular message. Tradition has a high appeal for a large audience. Tradition demands that all sins of the entire world were paid for. However, when a Christian is suffering from willful sin, the traditional pastor may <u>not</u> have an answer. Free will indoctrination has a favorable entrance, but an unknown explanation.

> **And he is the propitiation for our sins: and not for ours only, but also for** *the sins of* **the whole world.** I John 2:2

Privately interpreted or left to stand-alone by ignoring the rest of Scripture, the above verse is easily interpreted incorrectly. If this verse literally meant "*the sins of* **the whole world**" the sin of unbelief would be satisfied and unbelievers would be redeemed. Likewise, forgiving the unforgivable sin of blasphemy would be a problem (see Matt. 12:31). The punishment of sin toward the nation of Israel would be a problem (see Ezek. 39:23-24). The payment from Israel's punishment would be a problem (see Jer. 16:17-18). Willful sins by the Christian would be a problem (see Heb. 10:26). In this verse "**our sins**" applies to the elect Christians. Jesus paid for the sins of His elect on the cross in order to merit the new birth. The second word "*sins*" within "**but also** *for the sins of* **the whole world**" is <u>not</u> in the Greek text. If you look up the word "**sins**" in a concordance of the Bible you will notice that the second word "*sins*" within I John 2:2 is <u>not</u> in the original Greek (NIG). In the King James Version, "*the sins of*" is in italics, notifying the reader that these English words are <u>not</u> in the Greek text. A Greek word for English translation would be "**And he is the propitiation for our sins: and not for ours only, but also for the whole world**". In some contexts, the word "**world**" is simple the place where people live and I believe the word "**world**" in this context is the elect within all nations or ethnic groups of the world. The propitiation of the elect was not limited to one ethnic group, but all ethnic groups of the world.

However, the word "**world**" may imply that the cross had something to do with a future change in the natural world, but not for the propitiation of every sin of everyone in the world (see Rom. 8:19-22).

If you ask your pastor or Spiritual leader about this verse, he or she may include the *italics* as Scripture and support the traditional interpretation. In fact, the top-ten leaders of the top-ten denominations (one hundred educated and godly leaders) will probably state the cross dealt will all sins. Implying that all sins were forgiven at the cross is foundational for the free will advocates. Free will has appeal, support and strength in the American church.

However, I see in Scripture and contemporary life, where Christians can pay for his or her willful sin outside of the realm of the cross. For the Christian, virtually all sins were paid for or redeemed by the Blood of Jesus at the cross. However, Scripture should not be ignored where willful sins are paid for by judgment upon the Christian in this earthly life outside the realm of the cross. This does not imply that Christians renounce their salvation as a son or daughter of God (see Luke 15:11-32). Still, the Lord forbids sin with the presumption of blank consequences (see Rom. 5:1-2, 15-16). To illustrate, imagine a gift of a paid vacation to Hawaii, including travel, lodging, food and entertainment. Once there, you see a hat that you like and you use your own personal income to pay for the hat. The exotic hat is outside the realm of the gift. Likewise, Christians have a guarantee of reaching heaven, but the Christian pays for his or her willful sin through judgment in this present life on earth. God's judgments start here and now with Christians, while unbelievers are storing up wrath for the last day (see I Pet. 4:17; Rom.2:5).

Hebrews 10:26-31 testifies to a willful sin by a Christian in which there is no sacrifice in the cross of the Lord Jesus, but a judgment by the Lord. You could easily state that all sins were dealt with at the cross, but that would nullify or be problematic to this Scripture in Hebrews and others. For example, the apostle John testifies to a sin unto death (see I John 5:16). We have an example of this sin unto death by Ananias and his wife Sapphira, both appearing to be part of the church (see Acts 5:1-10). As believers, they sinned and died as judgment, but remained saved. Some believe that Satan deceives Christians to believe that there are sins that cannot be forgiven.[4] I believe Satan may have filled Ananias and Sapphira to believe that God would forgive their sin of lying using his old deception of, "**you shall not surely die**". Another example is a member of the Corinthian church that Paul said would remain saved on the day of the Lord even though Satan would destroy his flesh (see I Cor. 5:1-5). The Lord judged these Christians' willful sin and they were given the death sentence. The payment of sin was outside of the realm of the cross. These willful sins by the Christian are judged by God in the here and now. The most extreme judgment is physical death, although some denominations teach that the most extreme judgment is Spiritual separation, loss of salvation or backsliding.

Backsliding is returning to your former nature by severing your connection with God through sin and disobedience. You renounce your faith and transition from a state of grace back to a state of wrath. I am suspicious of backsliding because the goal appears to refrain church members from sinning. I have known church members that cherish the belief in backsliding and appear to treat "once saved, always saved" as a stumbling block. If the belief in backsliding is the primary reason that a church member refrains from returning to their old nature, they probably are exercising self-reformation, <u>not</u> Spiritual regeneration. Suffering by the Christian is the primary results of willful sins, <u>not</u> backsliding (see I Pet. 2:20a). Those who sin and do <u>not</u> suffer may be unsaved, <u>not</u> saved and backslidden (see Heb. 12:8). Those who sin and are saved, God will forgive or judge, but <u>not</u> separate them from his family.

Judgment for willful sin is <u>not</u> conditional salvation based upon obedience. There is no act of obedience to merit salvation and the Blood of the Lord Jesus was enough to atone for sins in order to authorize adoption as children of God. However, willful sins by the child of God are judged outside of the cross (see I Pet. 4:17a). This interpretation does <u>not</u> give a weak interpretation of Hebrews 10:26-31 and no change of Spiritual nature occurs. You do <u>not</u> renounce your salvation, since that is impossible (see Heb. 6:4). This is limited atonement.[5] The sin of the elect were paid for at the cross, but the willful sin of the elect are dealt with through suffering or physical death.

And almost all things are by the law purged with blood; and without shedding of blood is no remission. Heb. 9:22

The shedding of Blood is required for remission or forgiveness, but willful sins can be dealt with through judgment or death when forgiveness is <u>not</u> allowed (see Isa. 22:14, 40:2). The writer of Hebrews states that **almost all things are purged with Blood** (cross). Just because a sin is <u>not</u> purged with Blood, does <u>not</u> mean that it cannot be purged. Willful sins are purged or erased through judgment upon the Christian offender. This closes the door to the free will license. However, the people of God have a long history of rejecting Truths they are <u>not</u> comfortable with.

The Blood of Jesus was for a new covenant established at the heavenly altar, creating a new birth with a new heart and nature (see Matt. 26:28; Heb. 9). Only Jesus was able to redeem sinners for this. Jesus descended into hades in order to prevent the gates of hades from prevailing against His church or called-out ones (see Acts 2:27-31; Eph. 4:9; Matt. 16:18). Jesus changed the path after death.

Meanwhile, a son or daughter of God must bear his or her cross of suffering for willful sins in order to learn obedience (see Matt. 16:24; Heb. 5:8-9; I Pet. 4:1-2). What are willful sins? God knows. Yet a short list might include:

- Un-forgiveness toward others (Matt. 6:15)
- Lying to Holy Spirit (Acts 5:3-5)
- Unworthy participation during communion (I Cor. 11:28-30)
- Willful fornication (I Cor. 5:1-5)
- Covetous, idolatry, railing, drunkenness, extortion (I Cor. 5:11)
- Boastful ability (Matt. 20:21-23; 26:33-35)
- Disobedience to government (Rom. 13:1)

I do not include blasphemy against Holy Spirit in this short list because I do not believe a Christian can commit this sin. What is the judgment for willful sins? God knows. Yet a short line might include:

- Death
- Exclusion from fellowship
- Sickness
- Judgment from government (Rom. 13:2)

The apostle John states that there are sins not unto death (see I John 5:17). An example is seen in the unworthy participation during communion within the Corinthian church. Many were weak and sick because the Lord judged them outside the realm of forgiveness in the cross (see I Cor. 11:30).

A simplistic illustration would be the birth of a child to human parents. The child had nothing to do with the birth and is granted position in the family. Still, the parents should deal with disobedience. The child cannot appeal to his or her position in the family as merit for disobedience. The child might confess to his or her parents and ask forgiveness and avoid punishment for certain acts. For example, the child may break a vase, which the parents must pay to replace. However, other acts merit punishment in order to correct the willful disobedience. Do parents have a page in their book of house rules that forgives all acts of misconduct through confession? Why would the Lord chastise and scourge His children if their willful sins were all forgiven at the cross (see Heb. 12:4-10)? Why would the writer of Hebrews testify to Jesus as an example of suffering when we suffer (see Heb. 12:2-3)? Christians suffer for willful sins, which justify payment of these willful sins, just as Jesus suffered for payment for our redemption and change of nature.

> **For whom the Lord loveth he chasteneth,
> and scourgeth every son whom he receiveth.**
> Heb. 12:6

The word "**scourgeth**" in the Scripture above is the same Greek word "mastigoo" that Jesus used to describe His future suffering in Jerusalem (see Mark 10:34). And the same Greek word that the apostle John used to describe what Pilate did to Jesus (see John 19:1). The Lord was scourged for payment of our many sins, while Christians are scourged for payment of willful sins.

Not all suffering is due to willful sins. Living a godly life can bring suffering (see II Tim. 3:12). Martyrdom is the ultimate. Yet martyrdom could be a gift of the Spirit (see I Cor. 13:3). Remember the face of Stephen radiated as he spoke words of blessings while being stoned to death (see Acts 6:15, 7:55-60). The Lord has promised never to leave or forsake His people. Holy Spirit will put words in the Christian's mouth during these confrontations. All glory goes to God, even in martyrdom (see John 21:19).

However, willful sins bring suffering to the Christian, not the Savior. One of the most unscriptural songs about sin is "*Feel The Nails*" by Ray Boltz. The song asks, "*Does He still feel the nails every time I fail?*" No, Jesus does not feel the nails when we fail or sin. The payment was paid for once at the cross (see Heb. 10:14). We may feel the nails as we enter into suffering with Him in this life for our willful sins (see Phil. 3:10). Why did the apostle Peter have to suffer and die on a cross if all his sins were forgiven (see John 21:18)? Why did the apostle Paul, the chief sinner, bear in his body the marks of the Lord Jesus (see I Tim 1:15: Gal. 6:17)? Paul's faith was authored by the Lord to include sufferings for willful sins (see Acts 9:16; Heb. 12:2).

Willful sins are thought out and acted upon. Christians falsely assume forgiveness. Fifty years ago adultery was called adultery. Thirty years ago adultery was called an affair. Today, adultery has softened in the free will culture to just a date. Married Christians schedule their dates. This is willful sin based upon Scripture, <u>not</u> my judgment of others. They act this way because they believe that all their sins were paid for at the cross. Marriage is honorable, but adulterers God will judge, even His people (see Num. 25; Heb. 10:30, 13:4).

Man lives by every Word of God. Man errors by partials. Christians appeal privately to I John 1:9 for willful sins.

> **If we confess our sins, he is faithful and just to forgive us *our* sins, and to cleanse us from all unrighteousness.** I John 1:9

The Scripture above speaks of a salvation experience based upon the context. The previous verse 8 states "**the truth is not in us**" and the following verse 10 states "**His word is not in us**," implying someone without God. The typical sinner's prayer starts with confession of sin followed by believing that Jesus died for your sin (see Rom. 10:9). I John 1:9 describes a confession at salvation. Confessing is stating the same thing that God believes about sin. The unbeliever has received faith to believe. Therefore, I John 1:9 is a confession of salvation, <u>not</u> an appeal for willful sins. I John 1:9 is the umbrella Scripture at salvation while willful sins are the button you push to fold up the umbrella and receive judgment from God (see Heb. 10:26). Scripture states both "**all**" sins were forgiven and Scripture that states "**many**" sins were forgiven (see Rom. 5:16). At salvation all past and present sins were forgiven. After salvation, many sins that are <u>not</u> willful were forgiven at the cross and prayer and confession is possible (see Luke 11:4). Nevertheless, the Christian pays for willful sins from the judgment of God (whatever that may be), yet the Christian does <u>not</u> renounce his or her salvation.

Instead of assuming forgiveness, Christians can avoid suffering the judgment of God by avoiding willful sins. I was traditionally taught that all sins are forgiven through confession. This is true at salvation and for many sins, but those willful sins must be dealt with through judgment upon the Christian. This pictures a loving Father granting the gift of salvation and forgiveness in the daily walk, but <u>not</u> allowing willful sins; knowing that suffering will prevent continual sinning (see I Pet. 4:1). The Father is wise in His dealing with His children, <u>not</u> cruel, but corrective. Unlike a careless parent that lets the misdeeds escalate into permanent behavior, the Father's love will <u>not</u> allow His children to run wild. Meanwhile, a mature Christian can judge self (see I Cor. 11:31). For example, after telling a willful lie, the Christian may fast, bringing remorse to the soul.

This is strong meat for growth, <u>not</u> baby milk or junk food. This is a comprehensive interpretation considering all relevant Scripture. The Catholic Church hoovers over this principle with penances and purgatory, but lands outside the boundaries of Scripture with indulgences offered by the church from their storehouse of accumulated virtues. The traditional Protestant Church falsely assumes forgiveness as the only means to purge willful sins. And both groups have extreme non-ending punishment for the unsaved.

The Lord has established a new covenant to keep His people in line, but they perish in this earthly culture for lack of knowledge. Judgment for willful sins is a problem if you believe God has granted free will to His children. There is liberty with the Spirit of the Lord, but judgment begins at the house of God concerning willful sin. Later, judgment for the unsaved occurs in the lake of fire and they will be annihilated once the payment has been satisfied (see Ezek. 28:19, 43:8).

Suffering

Life would be grand without any suffering. Can you imagine snapping your finger every time you needed something? This may be a desire for man, but appears to be the opposite will of God. Faith needs a path of trials to strengthen the faith muscles in order for a child to grow toward a mature son or daughter of God.

The apostle Paul had a unique call to suffer and he implied that suffering is a part of the Christian life (see Acts 9:16). Suffering may be a window of time when we fellowship with Jesus (see Phil. 3:10). Jesus had an experience; a window of time, from the Mount of Olives to His last breath on the cross, where the Father and Spirit appeared passive and the powers of darkness stepped in (see Luke 22:52). Christians may experience times when Holy Spirit appears silent and the powers of this world are active. In Christ there is suffering as we are being conformed to His image. A common pattern that the Lord uses is to lead someone through a wide range of experiences, from suffering to exaltation. Does someone choose these experiences? No. Abraham was asked to sacrifice his son; then was greatly blessed. Job experienced tragedy and physical suffering, later to be greatly blessed in the end. Joseph was brought to the prison in Egypt; then promoted to second in command. The most prominent was God's beloved Son. He experienced the most severe rejection, humiliation and suffering; then He was exalted to the highest position of honor (see Phil. 2:9).

It is beyond our understanding to know why suffering happens in every situation. Please do <u>not</u> say that you understand to someone who has unexpectedly lost a loved one, unless you truly understand. Please do <u>not</u> ask them how their loved one died. Your presence will be appreciated, but your silence will be golden. It has been advised <u>not</u> to consider the cause, but to realize that "**unless you repent, you shall all perish**" (see Luke 13:3).

New Testament Prayer

The disciples struggled with prayer and asked Jesus for advice (see Luke 11:1). Prayer from a corrupt soul that has not been renewed with the Word of God can be selfish. Paul stated that we do not know how to pray as we ought, but Holy Spirit helps us (see Rom. 8:26). His Spirit within us will pray according to God's will, while the soul of man will pray according to self will. The Spirit within us will agree with the Word of God in our renewed mind and our prayers will be according to His will. When we pray, "**lead us not into temptation, but deliver us from evil**," we acknowledge the Spiritual robotics of the Lord over His creation (Matt. 6:13). Also, Holy Spirit has the ability to control our tongue and pray for us. The apostle James stated that the tongue is untamable by man (see Jam. 3:8). Praying in the Spirit is closer to a robotic action than an action initiated and controlled by man (see Jude 1:20). Meanwhile, silent prayers cannot be ruled out (see I Thes. 4:17). And there may be times when someone is too poor in spirit to speak (see Matt 5:3). Still, the Scripture states that vocal prayers are the standard (see Luke 11:2).

Prayer answered

One day I went to mow my mother's lawn. I prayed that the lawn mower would start on the first pull. I would often struggle starting the lawn mower. I primed it and trusted God to answer my prayer. I pulled the cord and nothing. So I pulled it again and again and still nothing. I paused for a minute and reflected on my prayer and had a moment of mediation. An idea came to replace the old gasoline. I turned the mover over, drained out the old gasoline and drove to the store and bought some new gasoline. I returned and poured the new gasoline in the mower and it started on the first pull. My prayer was answered through revelation. My will was for the mower to start on the first pull. The revelation from God let me know how to start the mower on the first pull. God is frugal to use existing resources rather than perform a miracle. This principle is in Scripture.

Mind

A Christian has a new Spiritual nature. The new nature has Holy Spirit as Guide, Comforter and Teacher. Holy Spirit operates in harmony with the Word of God. The human mind does not have the new nature. The renewing of the mind with the Word of God resolves this. The goal is to be Spiritually minded which is life and peace (see Rom. 8:6). Thinking with a carnal mind is the old nature. This is where the rubber meets the road, so to speak. The mind is the access switch between natures. You are not alone. You have been given faith (see I Pet. 1:5). The mark of faith is a high level of obedience. This is perfection. Along the path is suffering and joy as the Christian is being conformed to the image of Jesus (Phil. 3:10-15). Meanwhile, sin or missing the mark is its lowest level. It would be a rough definition of "free will" to place the responsibility of the Christian in determining which level of obedience he or she decides to roost on. The goal should be a mind renewed with the Word of God. Rare Spiritual robotics may follow.

Church Growth

Due to the exceptional freedom of worship in America, the glory of God has been compromised to a vision of large attendance. Not so in Scripture. Instead God is gloried when His people are obedient, even to death by martyrdom (see John 21:19).

From my experience, most pastors want and expect their church to grow in membership. The pastor believes he is doing everything he can to facilitate growth by being a faithful witness and preaching the Word. And the members believe they are being obedient in their witnessing, tithing and study of the Word. Yet when growth is not happening the pastor may assume it is the members' short comings; and likewise the members may assume it is the pastor's short coming. Both may be wrong. They do <u>not</u> like to consider that God determines growth (see I Cor. 3:7). The book of Acts hints at church growth, but the gospels and the epistles do <u>not</u> appear to expect growth (see Acts 2:41, 47). Individual Christian maturity and growth is expected, but *"getting the numbers up"* is a worldly philosophy (see II Pet. 3:18). The Scriptures testify to a remnant (see Isa. 1:9), a few (see Deut. 7:7), a little flock (see Luke 12:32) and salt (see Matt. 5:13) which is a small quantity (God's family) amidst the larger quantity (world population). Church growth may occur, but credit belongs to the Lord. And I do <u>not</u> rule out the faithfulness of the pastor and the members.

However, the Lord is looking for an environment where His children can grow. I have experienced two swings. 1) The leader(s) exercise too much control that leads to bondage and discouragement and 2) the leader(s) allow too much sin in the camp. Both can prevent the blessings of God and hinder church growth.

A pastor is a shepherd. The role of a pastor is to comfort, feed and lead. Sometimes the pastor attempts to herd the sheep. The message can be wrong, attempting to force the sheep to witness using guilt and shame. The sheep do <u>not</u> hear these voices and will flee (see John 10:5). Perhaps this explains the decrease in church attendance in certain areas? Perhaps the growth in other areas is due to a ministry of comfort and encouragement instead of control and manipulation? The message should be what Jesus has done and what He can do through His church, <u>not</u> what we can do for Jesus using our wills. A church usually follows one of two directions: growth from God or control by men.

Below are a few issues to growth that I have observed:

- Traditional doctrine that does <u>not</u> line up with Scripture.
- Church staff member(s) practicing open marriage with acceptance.

- Pastor hostile toward church member(s) demonstrating superior Bible knowledge during open discussions.
- Pastor with a bossy attitude.

Christians go to church to be encouraged and hear the Word preached (see Heb. 10:25). I personally need a double dose of the Word. I struggle with fifteen to twenty minutes of announcements and thirty to forty minutes of songs. Some Christians do not go to church and I cannot be sure that it is their shortcomings (see Col. 2:16). Un-churched Christians need encouragement (see Heb. 10:24-25).

Church Initiated Programs

The church consists of members that primarily live outside the realm of the church building. Often the only ministry that is recognized are those which the leader(s) of the church initiate within the realm of the church building. For example, singing in the choir, teaching Sunday school, visitation, soup kitchen, etc. These are important, but are not inclusive of the entire ministry of the church. For example, a member may make a godly business decision that the Lord sees, but is invisible to the eyes and ears of the local congregation. A member may encourage someone in the check-out-line at the grocery store. The local church ministry is broader than the recognizable ministries at the church. The silent majority of ministry may be performed outside the recognition of the announced visible ministry. Churches often narrow it to a few hours of programs initiated by the church, instead of the 24/7-day a week ministry in the work place, market place and home. Due to an emphasis on church initiated programs such as praise, evangelism and other recognizable acts, some members are ignored:

- The weak are not strengthen (see Ezek. 34:4).
- The sick are not healed.
- The broken are not bandaged.

- Those driven away are <u>not</u> brought back or sought for.
- The sinful are <u>not</u> disciplined.

The primary programs are encouragement and edification. Members need power to do their daily tasks at home, work or elsewhere. Church programs can be burdens when assigned to someone who is <u>not</u> called to that program (see Acts 6:2). Joy can be experienced when a church program is properly assigned. Meanwhile, a member may feel guilty if they deny a program. There should be a mutual agreement between God, the leader(s) and the member(s) in the assignment of church programs. However, the main thing is the broad reach of daily tasks by the members outside the church walls, although church leader(s) do <u>not</u> always acknowledge ministry unless it's under their watchful eyes.

Church Sermons

Some churches do <u>not</u> know how to encourage. They assume you need to be corrected and scolded. I have heard many sermons where the Preacher lays a foundation that identifies the congregation as having missed the mark, failed to perform or disobeyed. Then he or she shifts to exhorting the congregation to do better, try harder or confess and start over. The assumption is to do better, but the message does <u>not</u> consider that some members may be doing excellent. This is similar to a teacher taking up the students' test papers and presumptuously stating, "*I know no one made a 100. All of you need to study harder.*"

The opposite message exists in other churches. They sound more like a political message of prosperity, health and blessings. The exhortations are always in the future tense, such as "*God is going to pour out a mighty move of the Holy Ghost.*" At first, I believed these messages, but after many years of hearing the same exhortations repeated again and again, I became suspicious.

Meanwhile, sermons often note the faith of an Old Testament or New Testament character and exhort the congregation to do likewise. These sermons can be frustrating as the hearer tries to muster up and do something they are not called and not equipped to do. They are left with the guilt of being inadequate to accomplish a great work for God. Bible characters glorify God who imparts faith, but sermons often praise the character. Bible characters are examples, but like-faith with the same results can rarely be exhorted from a message about the character. Like-faith of a Bible character is usually the will of the preacher for the church members to copy. Paul said it is not wise to compare one to another because God has given a measure of faith, individually as He pleases (see II Cor. 10:12; Rom. 12:3).

Meanwhile, faith will come as the Word (Jesus) is preached. The faith from God is an individual and unique impartation of the will of God. You cannot copy a past work of God by duplicating the acts to "make it happen". You are a chosen generation, not a repeat of yesterday (see I Pet. 2:9).

Please note that the above minor observation of church programs and sermons does not include the majority of things that are well pleasing to the Lord. My goal is to encourage change in the things that are not.

Spirit Filled

There are many sermons about the need to be filled with the Spirit, but few describe how to be filled (see Eph. 5:18). Usually the preacher exhorts the congregation to be filled with the Spirit while remaining silent about how. Holy Spirit fillings involve more of not doing than doing because Holy Spirit does what He wants to do (see Acts 1:2). In the book of Acts, the disciples were to wait (see Acts 1:4). Later, the apostle(s) would baptize in the Spirit (see Acts 19:6). From observation, the below list may help:

- Church attendance
- Ask (prayer)

- Stop reasoning
- Be still and quiet
- Be humble and submissive
- Cease eating
- Repent or be wise in obedience (see Eph. 5:17)
- Sing (see Eph. 5:19)
- Man of God to minister fillings

Opinion

God does care about your opinion. Jesus asked His disciples their opinion of who He was (see Matt. 16:15-16). Opinions were given. Only Peter got it right due to a revelation from the Father (see 16:17).

Money

You will be responsible for what you have been given and what you have been called to do. Some folks do <u>not</u> understand how money works. They have a poor credit rating. Financial institutions will <u>not</u> loan them money because his or her credit rating shows that they do <u>not</u> understand how money works. They have been deceived by free will without consequences. However, some have poor credit due to circumstances beyond their control. The flow of money can be illustrated by the flow of water in a river. You can stop the flow by <u>not</u> paying your bills and <u>not</u> supporting others in a proper way.

Salvations are contingent on God alone. It is <u>not</u> wise to believe that money can translate into salvations. Yes, money is needed to support evangelical outreach, but it is <u>not</u> wise to believe that the number of salvations will be contingent on the amount of money given. Ministries falsely appeal for money for Spiritual results. One pastor announced that he had asked God for a million in the Kingdom as a result of giving at his local church, which sponsored many outreach efforts. One ministry newsletter stated, *"He is using your generosity to draw men and women to Christ."* Another stated, *"What are you willing to give to see souls saved*?" In the natural, money appears to translate into salvations, but Scripture states differently (see Acts 8:20). Is money so important? If given one wish, would you ask to be the richest, wisest, powerful, fairest, healthiest, happiest or most obedient person in the world?

Come On

What does "*Come On*" mean? Did "*Come On*" originate in secular concerts? Yet I hear "*Come On*" from Christian musicians and praise team leaders. I am <u>not</u> sure what "*Come On*" means or to whom the exhortation is directed: God, self or the audience? I assume the audience is passive and needs to become active in worship or move higher in praise. Please. Could the exhorter of the "*Come On*" explain to the congregation exactly what he or she wanted them to do or to whom it was directed? Here is a line from a song by the Impressions "*Come on, Savior, change my behavior.*" This may be a petty issue, but I do <u>not</u> like starting a Christian service with a secular exhortation. The Scriptures identify evil and blessings in this exhortation (see Gen 44:34; Gal. 3:14).

Television and Movies

Television can be a source of edification or an avenue of evil. Long sessions can sunburn your heart. Television can make you like a parrot, repeating words without knowing the philosophy behind them. Instead of Scripture, people often reference movies and television to explain life. Beware. There are people on television "*spitting out a bunch of words just to see where they will land.*"[6] Robotics is a popular analogy used in television and in the culture. On February 2, 2012 on the O'Reilly Factor, a woman was arrested the following Saturday, January 28, 2012 in Oakland, California for protesting in the "Occupy" movement. She described police activity as "*many instances of cruelty from what appeared to be robotic monster type people.*"

I do not go to the movies in theatres. Instead, I have written to my congressman that the movie industry should be taxed, similar to alcohol and tobacco for its detrimental effect on the culture. For example:

- R   7%
- PG-13   5%
- PG   3%
- G   0%

Chapter Twelve

Blessings

If you believe that you are blessed because you are well liked, popular, rich and happy, the Words of Jesus may <u>not</u> find agreement in your heart (see Matt. 5:1-12). Instead, you are blessed when the Words of Jesus finds agreement in your heart (see John 20:29). You are blessed when you receive revelation from God (see Matt. 16:17). You are blessed when you read the book of Revelation (see Rev. 1:3).

> Praise God, from Whom all blessings flow;
> Praise Him, all creatures here below;
> Praise Him above, ye heavenly host;
> Praise Father, Son and Holy Ghost.

What are blessings? Blessings are favorable words, deeds and/or provisions that aid others. Man can bless man and man can bless God (see Matt. 5:44; Jam. 3:9). This chapter focuses on blessings from God to man. Below is a partial list.

Material or Money

After stepping out of my Ford F-150 truck at Bible College, one of the students said, *"The Lord has put His blessings on you with that truck."* Indeed, the soul and body of God's servants prosper from material provisions (see Phil. 4:18-19; III John 2).

> **And the Lord hath blessed my master greatly; and he is become great: and he hath given him flocks, and herds, and silver, and gold, and menservants, and maidservants, and camels, and asses.** Gen. 24:35

When you do what you want or free will, money is your master (see Matt. 6:24). Money is a good servant, but a bad master.[1] Scripture warns about material blessings. Material blessings can lead man to believe that his self-efforts obtained wealth (see Deut. 8:17). When Jesus walked with His disciples on earth, the Jews recognized wealth as the supreme blessing because their covenant was earthly (see Deut. 28). Wealth is a by-product of obedience to the law of God on earth, but unrelated to the future inheritance in heaven. The disciples of Jesus were disturbed when Jesus said that it is easier for a camel to go through the eye of a needle than for a rich man to enter the Kingdom of heaven (see Matt. 19:24). Jesus described riches as briers that choke the Word from the heart of man (see Mark 4:19). The apostle Paul said that the love of money is the root of all evil (see I Tim. 6:10). When you love God will all your heart, no place exists for the love of money (see Eph. 4:27).

The earth is the Lord's and the fullness thereof; the world, and they that dwell therein (Ps. 24:1). Satan is <u>not</u> the owner of this world. Satan is described as "**the god of this world**" or of this time-limited world philosophy (see II Cor. 4:4). Indeed, Satan offered Jesus the kingdoms of this world, but can the father of lies deliver (see Matt. 4:8-9; John 8:44)? Satan's job title is to steal, kill and destroy (see John 10:10). Therefore, material provisions can be fuel the enemy uses to entice sin (see Matt. 4:9; Jam. 1:13-14). Material blessings from God can be a window where Satan tries to satisfy his appetite of deception and destruction. The Lord gives money to bless while Satan uses money to control. Nevertheless, money is needed in this current world system to accomplish the will of the Father. However, a robot of Jesus has no room in his or her heart for covetous thoughts, words or deeds.

Forgiveness

God regretted that He had made man, but also pitied man. Instead of destroying man, God chose to manifest His blessings on man. Forgiveness is a blessing from God (see Ps. 103). The Blood of Jesus can purge sin from God's remembrance and from man's consciousness where neither God nor man remembers the evil (see Heb. 9:14,10:2, 22). A robot of Jesus has no place in his or her heart for un-forgiveness.

Peace (soul)

Peace is a calm emotion state of the soul, an absence of anxiety and a sense of well-being.

> **Thou wilt keep him in perfect peace, whose mind is stayed on thee: because he trusteth in thee.** Isa. 26:3

Anxiety occurs when man uses his natural senses (touch, sight and hearing) while observing disturbances or hearing disturbing words. A list could be made of disturbances and spoken words that eliminate peace (see Gen. 3:10; Dan. 5:5-6; Matt. 8:26). A psychologist may wonder if anxiety is due to your parent's DNA or from the circumstances in life or a combination of both? God knows (see II Tim. 1:5; Heb. 4:13). Man does not know because peace is not observable within the soul; only the behavior of man is observable.

The world does not provide peace without a price. Peace must be obtained through prayer, sacrifice, suffering, self-denial and wisdom (see Jam. 3:13-4:7). Selfish ambitions can eliminate peace (see Jam. 4:1). Jesus came preaching repentance from selfish ambitions in order for the soul and culture to thrive in peace. This involves loving the Lord and neighbor, which brings a culture closer to the kingdom of peace in heaven (see Mark 12:34). A list could be made of how peace is obtained.

- The Lord will bless His people with peace (see Ps. 29:11).
- Jesus provided peace with the Father (see John 14:27).
- Individual and national peace through prayer (see Phil. 4:6-7; I Tim 2:1-2).
- Fruit of the Spirit (see Gal. 5:22).
- A spouse from the Lord (see Gen. 2:18; Prov. 31:10-12, 28).

Ultimately, Jesus is the Prince or Ruler of peace. He is the only way to obtain lasting peace by changing the corrupt soul from Adam into a Spiritual nature (see Eph. 1:2-3). A robot of Jesus is full of peace with no room for fear, anxiety or anger (see I John 4:18).

Health (body)

There is a connection between a peaceful soul and a healthy body. Health is a strong and well-functioning physical body. Jesus healed physical illnesses in order to bless people and confirm His calling (see Luke 13:16; John 7:31). Jesus still heals.

> **And the very God of peace sanctify you wholly; and** *I pray God* **your whole Spirit and soul and body be preserved blameless unto the coming of our Lord Jesus Christ. Faithful** *is* **he that calleth you, <u>who also will do</u>** *it*. I Thes. 5:23-24

Notice that Jesus does it (see underline above). He starts in the Spirit from the very God of peace. Next, the fruit of the Spirit sustains the soul, which sustains a healthy body. Remember, man lives by faith (Spirit). You live in the natural world due to a healthy body. Therefore, health is a blessing from God. However, a robot of Jesus will experience a decline in the body as his or her soul nears separation (see II Cor. 5:1).

Control (Spirit)

Natural man cannot fully control his carnal desires and cannot fully obey the law of God (see Gen. 3 -Rev. 20). Natural man is like a one directional (stiff-necked) robot headed toward ruin (see Rom. 3:10-18). Nevertheless, God is rich in grace and controls the transition of the natural man to a Spiritual (born again) nature. Jesus sent Holy Spirit in order to flip the control from the natural to the Spiritual, from earth to heaven (see Eph. 1:3). The purpose of Holy Spirit is to bless regenerated man with the control from heaven. The purpose of Scripture is to harmonize the mind with the will of God.

The free will of man in the natural world is part of God's plan. Freedom is better than bondage to another (see I Cor. 7:21). I am not against choice, but human choices are flawed. Man's freedom to make choices is not always a blessing (see Ps. 1). The least recognized and most important blessing from God is control. A popular allegorical text by a disputed author illustrates this.

Footprints in the Sand

> One night I had a dream. . . I dreamed I was walking along the beach with the Lord, and Across the sky flashed scenes from my life. For each scene I noticed two sets of footprints in the sand; One belonged to me, and the other to the Lord. When the last scene of my life flashed before us, I looked back at

the footprints in the sand. I noticed that many times along the path of my life, There was only one set of footprints. I also noticed that it happened at the very lowest and saddest times in my life. This really bothered me, and I questioned the Lord about it. "Lord, you said that once I decided to follow you, You would walk with me all the way; But I have noticed that during the most troublesome times in my life, There is only one set of footprints. I don't understand why in times when I needed you the most, you should leave me." The Lord replied, "My precious, precious child. I love you, and I would never, never leave you during your times of trial and suffering. When you saw only one set of footprints, It was then that I carried you."

God can unconditionally control man, which is necessary in rare situations (see Rom. 8:5-9; Acts 2:4). This glories God and humbles man. Man cannot control Holy Spirit (see I Cor. 12:11). However, Holy Spirit can control the Spiritual man to speak and act according to the will of the Father (see Matt. 10:20). This divine control is <u>not</u> boring or mundane, but joyful and exciting. This is rare Spiritual robotics. Still, natural and Spiritual men are responsible for their words and deeds when this divine control is relaxed and when the soul of man must choose. A relaxed state is more common although it does <u>not</u> negate the rare. When this rare divine control is exercised the individual is <u>not</u> responsible, all glory goes to God, but afterward the individual becomes more responsible due to the revelation of this ability from God (see II Cor. 12:7).

Praise the Lord Who can open a window in heaven and pour into the heart of man, faith that can accomplish great deeds for His glory. These deeds are recorded in Scripture, such as Elijah's rapture into heaven (see II Kings 2:11). These deeds are recorded in church history, such as the revivals by

John Wesley, George Whitefield and others. These deeds are often credited in err to men and women, but they are rare Spiritual robotics. These controls from heaven are blessings that are poured out from the Father above (see Jam. 1:17).

> God bless America,
> Land that I love,
> Stand beside her and guide her
> Thru the night with a light from above;
> — Irving Berlin

New and Improved man: Robot of Jesus

The body of man was formed from the dust of the earth, while the soul of man was brought to life from the breath of God. Adam disobeyed and the soul and the blood became corrupt. Now everyone has a spirit, soul and body. The unsaved have a dead spirit towards God. With their conscience (soul), the unsaved can obey the laws of God to a limited degree. The Lord desires this (see II Pet. 3:9). This is repentance. Repentance allows man to live physically and <u>not</u> die physically from sin in the natural world. The Lord desires this even though repentance does <u>not</u> sway His will for His chosen elect in the Spiritual world (see Acts 9:1-6). Man can turn from sin toward God, but his sinful nature has <u>not</u> changed and he will eventually perish. In the Old Testament, the Lord made covenants with man based upon His law. These covenants were honored by God, but broken by man due man's inability to repent and obey God at a high level (see Matt. 23:37; Acts 15:10). Without intervention and control, man cannot operate as a robot of Jesus. Only a robot of Jesus can sustain permanent life.

God continued to work on man by imparting faith into Abraham, who demonstrated a high level of obedience. Abraham is called the father of faith (see Rom. 4:11-16). Now God takes this faith model and places faith into His children. Through Abraham's faith model, chosen individuals within all nations are blessed with a new heart (see Gen. 12:3; Gal. 3:8). This is another act of creation based solely upon the choice of God and not upon any act of man.

Therefore if any man *be* **in Christ,** *he* **is a new creation, old things are passed away: behold, all things are become new** (II Cor. 5:17).

Holy Spirit provides ability and revelation where the believer can see beyond the darkness of this world and operate with a hope for the coming of a righteous world. A robot can illustrate this Spiritual nature to a limited degree. A robot does not miss the mark or sin when given commands. A robot is an awkward analogy to describe this indescribable new creation. Quite frankly, my natural soul desired to abandon the robot analogy, but the Spiritual nature did not concur.

But as it is written, Eye hath not seen, nor ear heard, neither have entered into the heart of man, the things which God hath prepared for them that love him. But God hath revealed them unto us by his Spirit: for the Spirit searcheth all things, yea, the deep things of God. I Cor. 2:9-10

Man is blessed because His Creator is blessed and in control (see Eph. 1:3). If the Lord was not in control and the free will of man was honored without restraints, man would not be blessed. A robot of Jesus is blessed by the control from His Creator. The ultimate blessing is the Kingdom of God. In heaven, the new creation will be the removal of the corrupt blood and soul with its will to sin. The new creation will be a Spirit and an incorruptible body. This blessing is near.

Alleluia: for the Lord God omnipotent reigneth. Let us be glad and rejoice, and give honour to him: for the marriage of the Lamb

is come, and his wife hath made herself ready. Rev. 19:6b-7

Conclusion

Are you a natural person, a disciple or a robot of Jesus? What are you controlled by — this world, your flesh, free will or the blessed Word of God?

About the Author

John McCann works as a computer programmer in Augusta, Georgia and may be contacted at rarespiritualrobotics@gmail.com. Comments about errors in spelling, grammar and material too personal, too critical or unscriptural will be appreciated. Please include the page number(s).

Search "Rare Spiritual Robotics" for Video Trailer on YouTube / Facebook.

Endnotes

Introduction

[1] I am a five-point Calvinist. Also, I believe in conditional immortality (annihilation of the unsaved) and the administration of all the gifts of Holy Spirit for the church today. I am sensitive to the consciences of others who believe differently, while making a sincere attempt to interpret Scripture.

[2] Keith Moore, Faith Life Church/Moore Life Ministries, Mar. 11, 2012

[3] "Man/men" are used to imply both male(s) and female(s).

[4] (Vine's Complete Expository Dictionary, W.E Vine, Merrill F. Unger, William White, Jr. Thomas Nelson, 1996, page 594 NT)

[5] God's Perfect Child: Living and Dying in the Christian Science Church, Caroline Fraser, Holt Paperbacks, August 1, 2000.

[6] www.Christianscience.com What is Christian Science?/About the Faith/Common confusions

Chapter One: Junk Food For The Soul

[1] Song; *Look Over The Beautiful Fields*, Joe Isaacs

[2] Noah Webster, American Dictionary of the English Language, Published by the Foundation for American Christian Education, San Francisco, California, 1995, Volume I, 88

[3] Peyton stated, "These circumstances; they are not the way either of us wish they were." Jim Irsay, stated, "we both wanted to be together."

[4] Noah Webster, American Dictionary of the English Language, Published by the Foundation for American Christian Education, San Francisco, California, 1995, Volume I, 46

[5] Merriam Webster's Collegiate Dictionary, Merriam-Webster, Philippines, 1993, page 943

[6] Luther and Erasmus: Free Will and Salvation, Editors: E. Gordon Rupp and Philip S. Watson, The Westminster Press, 1969, page 193

[7] Reinhold Nieburh (1892-1971)

[8] Experiment may not be the correct word. We know that God does test us. In the days of Noah, man was given a failing grade.

[9] Latif Yahia, The Black Hole: The Real Story of the Man Who Was Forced to Become The Double Of Saddam Hussein's Sadistic Son, Arcanum Media Group, 2006, page 3

[10] Jesse Duplantis, JDM Television Outreach, 2011

[11] Taylor, Cynthia, The Augusta Chronicle, August 2, 2013, http://chronicle.augusta.com/life/your-faith/2013-08-02/new-school-year-jesus-offers-fresh-starts

[12] Geisler, Norman L and Howe, Thomas, The Big Book of Bible Difficulties, Baker Books, Grand Rapids, Michigan, 1992, page 9

[13] The MacArthur Study Bible, NKJV large print, John MacArthur, editor, Word Publishing, a division of Thomas Nelson, 1997, page 1437

Chapter Two: The Disputed Border

[1] Whosoever Will, David L. Allen and Steve W. Lemke, B&H Publishing Group, Nashville, TN, 2010, page 29

[2] The Institution of the Christian Religion, John Calvin, edited by John T. McNeill, Westminster John Knox Press, Louisville/London, volume 2, 1960, page 921

Chapter Three: The Analogy of a Robot

[1] The King James Study Bible, Thomas Nelson, Inc., 1988, page 873

[2] a) Against Calvinism, Robert E. Olson, Zondervan, 2011, page 103. This is based upon reprobates.

b) The Spiritual Man, Watchman Nee, Christian Fellowship Publishers, New York, combined edition 1977, vol. II pages 63-65, vol. III 23, 95, 110.

[3] The theological term, hard determinism, exists in activation, although hard determinism does not exist in beautification. Hard determinism implies that man resists and God forces. The word "hard" is a stretch of the resistant ability of man. It

may not be a hard effort, but an easy motion with a passive subject. This may be soft determinism, but the bottom line is that God initiates, controls and accomplishes through man. How He does it, I do not know. These terms (hard determinism, etc.) are helpful, but not comprehensive (see Isa. 55:8; Rom. 11:34).

[4] See *commands* and *commandments* in the concordance of the New Testament. This is not legalism, but faith manifested by activity of Holy Spirit in a believer's life.

[5] The MacArthur Study Bible, NKJV large print, John MacArthur, editor, Word Publishing, a division of Thomas Nelson, 1997, page 1585

[6] God sometimes takes away all other choices. God did not force Jonah to go to Assyria, but Jonah did not have any other choice (see Jonah 2). The prodigal son did not have to return to his father, but he had no other choice (see Luke 15:17).

[7] Polk, Igor (2005-11-16). "RoboNexus 2005 robot exhibition virtual tour". Robonexus Exhibition 2005. Retrieved by Wikipedia 2007-09-10

[8] Psychology, ninth edition, David G. Myers, Worth Publishers, New York, NY, 2010, page 88

[9] Skydog - The Duane Allman Story, Randy Poe, Backbeat books, 2006, page 216-217

[10] The Cost of Discipleship, Dietrich Bonhoeffer, A Touchstone Book Published by Simon & Schuster, 1995, page 159

[11] What is the image of God in man? The final image will be at the end of time. Still, God is identified with a heart (Gen. 6:5), hand (Ps. 89:13), foot, finger, eyes, arm and face. Others believe this was when the Lord breathed into man and man

was given an immortal soul. I disagree with the immortal soul at the initial creation of man, since the Lord kept man away from the tree of life, lest he be like God and exist permanently or become immortal (see Gen. 3:22; I Cor. 15:54; I Tim. 6:16). The immortal soul concept is a prerequisite for evangelistic messages, such as "where you going to spend eternity?"

Chapter Four: Old Testament Robots

[1] The Zondervan Pictorial Encyclopedia of the Bible, The Zondervan Corporation, Grand Rapids, Michigan, 1975,1976, volume 4, page 375

[2] The New Defender's Study Bible, Henry Morris, World Publishing, Nashville, TN, 1995, 2006, pages 2042-2043

Chapter Six: Robots in Reverse

[1] Turning Point with David Jeremiah, Freedom Fighters

[2] A More Excellent Way, Henry Wright, Whitaker House, New Kensington, PA, 2009, page 148

[3] Brother Swaggart, Here is my question. . . Jimmy Swaggart, World Evangelism Press, 2009, page 151

[4] The New Greek-English Interlinear New Testament, Translators: Robert K. Brown and Philip W. Comfort, Editor: J.D. Douglas, Tyndale House Publishers, Inc., Wheaton, Illinois, 1990, page 768

[5] The Spirit of the Reformation Study Bible, Zondervan, 2003, page 2177

[6] The God Shaped Brain, Timothy R. Jennings, IVP, 2013, pages 211-219

[7] Family Medical Guide Volume One, page 113

[8] A TREASURY OF CHASSIDIC TALES – ON THE FESTIVALS VOL. II, 1982, by MESORAH PUBLICATIONS, Ltd. 1969 Coney Island Avenue / Brooklyn, N.Y. 11223 http://www.jewishbktown.com/st/Jewish_inspirational_books_stories_A_Treasury_of_Chassidic_Tales_vol_1.htm

[9] The literal words "soul" and "soulish" are placed in parenthesis. See the Darby or the Amplified translation of Lev. 17:11. See the Expanded Bible (EXB) translation of I Cor. 15:44. Scholars are disturbed with I Cor. 15:44 because they do not want to back off of the immortality of the soul.

[10] The God Shaped Brain, Timothy R. Jennings, IVP, 2013, page 70

Chapter Seven: The Wiring and Currency of Denominations

[1] Martin Luther: A Life, Martin E. Marty, Penguin book; reprint edition (August 26, 2008), page 68

[2] Reformation Time Line, Rose Publishing, 2006.

[3] Institutes of the Christian Religion, John Calvin, Westminster John Knox Press, volume 1, 1960, page 130.

[4] Why Evolution Is True, Jerry A. Coyne, Oxford University Press, 2009, page 248

Chapter Eight: Gospel Robots

[1] Gospel Truth with Andrew Wommack, October 6, 2011. An email reply from the ministry stated that Andrew emphasizes how serious the rejection of Christ is.

[2] Operation World, Patrick Johnstone and Jason Mandryk, WEC International, 2001, page 556

Chapter Nine: A Desire for Robots

[1] In Touch Ministry, Charles Stanley, "Why Did Jesus Have To Die?" April 2, 2012

Chapter Ten: Natural Robots

[1] Wheat Belly, William Davis, MD, Rodale, 2011, page 14

[2] The New Defender's Study Bible, KJV, Henry Morris, World Publishing, Inc., Nashville, TN, 1995, 2006, pages 811, 823, 1171

[3] God allows speculation (see Matt. 16:15; I Cor. 7:25). The rainbow or kaleidoscopic sky is speculation from Christian Life School of Theology course: BIBT542: Let There Be Light: Creationism, Rev. Timothy Robinson. After the flood of Noah, the rainbow in the sky appeared when God brought a cloud. The rainbow was to remind God, not man (see Gen. 9:12-16). God remembered how He had created the world initially with a rainbow sky that mirrored the rainbow above His throne in heaven (see Ezek. 1:18; Rev. 4:3). After the flood, the partial rainbow was a "**token**" of the covenant, similar to water in baptism and bread/wine in communion. Also consider that a possible rainbow mark on Cain's forehead may have let the people know that the Lord "above" was aware of Cain's actions (see Gen. 4:15; Rev. 10:1). Again this is speculation, which can appear impossible from man's perspective, but nothing is impossible with God.

[4] The Hebrew-Greek Key Study Bible, KJV, 1984 by Spiros Zodhiates and AMG International, Inc., page 1615

[5] The MacArthur Study Bible, NKJV large print, John MacArthur, editor, Word Publishing, a division of Thomas Nelson, 1997, page 1311

Chapter Eleven: Auxiliary Parts

[1] Power Rangers, Doctor K, season 17, episode 22

[2] The Spirit of the Reformation Study Bible, Zondervan, 2003, page 343

[3] The Catechism Explained, Spirago-Clarke, Tan Books and Publishers, Inc., 1993, page 143

[4] Lutzer, Erwin, The Serpent of Paradise, 1996, page 143

[5] Limited atonement is point three of the TULIP acrostic within Calvinism or Reformed Theology.

[6] The Comancheros (movie), 1961, John Wayne

Chapter Twelve: Blessings

[1] Frances Bacon, Sr. English Lawyer and Philosopher (1581-1626)

Index of Scripture

The Old Testament

Genesis
1:1 .... 69, 190	3:22 235
1:6-7 186	3:22-24 .... 123, 135
1:12 184	4:7 199
1:21 184	4:10 137
1:24-25 184	4:15 237
1:26a 70-71	5:24 .... xii, 62
1:26 24	6-8 37
1:27 viii	6:5 .... 83, 135, 139, 166, 234
1:29-30 188	6:5-6 25
1:31 186	6:5-7 84
2:7 ..... 21, 36, 66, 123-124, 134	6:7-8 139
2:16-17 19	6:8 83
2:17 81	6:13 81
2:18 222	6:22 .... 61, 197
3:1 186	7 184
3:1-7 36	7:11 187
3:5 81	7:11b 188
3:6 .... 19, 196	8:21 83
3:7 66	9:2 190
3:10 .... 77, 221	9:3 189
3:14-19 36	9:12-16 237
3:17b 188	11:1-9 .... 37, 50-51
3:19b 19	11:7-8 x

11:9 .... 61, 94
12:3 226
14:21 xii
15:13 87
17:1 84
19:13 81
19:24 188
19 60
20:6 x
22:1-18 28
22:10-18 84
22:11-12 21
24:35 220
39:9 87
44:34 217
50:15-21 135
50:19 87

Exodus
4:21 87
4 62
11:9 87
12:41 87
14:21 188
20:7 115
20:12 180
20:16 151
32:1-14 87
32:10-14 198
34:34-35 131

Leviticus
4:20-35 108
17:11a 136
17:11 .... 133, 236
17:11-14 190
18:22 151

26 95

Numbers
14:40-45 120
22:28 190
25 207
25:11 124

Deuteronomy
4:19 184
4:38 93
6:5 79
6:16 93
7:7 212
8:17 220
9:3 125
18:15-18 87
28 .... 81, 95, 108, 220
29:2-4 82
29:29 197
30:19 82
31:29 82
32:20 82
32:28 93

Joshua
24:15a 32
24:19a 32
24:19 88,137

Judges
2:7-13 82
2:17 82
2:20 93
3:10 82
6:12 88
6:36-40 88

Index of Scripture

7:15 88
11:29-40 141

Ruth
2:4 195

1 Samuel
3:1b 91
3:19 91
8:7 142
8:21-22 91
10:9 92
12:15-23 x
13:14 92
15:3 94
24:6 92

2 Samuel
7:8-9 92
11 92

1 Kings
17:4 190

2 Kings
2:11 224
23:13 30

Nehemiah
12:27 90

Esther
4:14 91
5:14-7:10 90

Job
1:1 85
1:8 85
1:13-19 174
1:22 85
2:7 174
14:5b 181
30:29 186
38-41 x
38:34 185
38:35-41 185
39 189
40:15 186
42:7-8 86

Psalms
1 223
1:2 66
2 xii
2:2-4 93
2:3 58
8:6 19
8:6-8 25
14:1a 198
23:3 136
23:3-4 137
23:6 82
24:1 220
29:11 222
37:4 29
51:17 132
89:13 234
91:11 21
103 221
103:8-9 121
104:35 124
105:25 51
115:3 vii
141:3-4a 92

Proverbs
1:29-33	198
2:16	175
3:5b	viii
3:5-6	104
3:5-7	30
11:22	175
11:30	135, 190
16:5	151
20:24	x
23:14	136
25:18	151
26:11	190
28:26	29
31:10-12	222
31:28	222

Ecclesiastes
1:2-3	30
11:5	27, 37
12:7	124
12:13-14	30-31

Isaiah
1:4	93
1:4-6	135
1:9	212
1:19	108
1:19-20	81
2:1-5	192
6	89
6:9	81
10:5	94
11	192
13:9	128, 146
13:14	54
19:25	94
22:14	204
26:3	221
40:2	204
40:31	50, 55, 148
43:7	63
43:13	105
52:1	63
53:1	43
55:8	67, 234
55:11	97
61:11	55
63:11	82
63:17	53
64:8	viii, 53
65:11	195

Jeremiah
9:2	177
9:23-24	198-199
11:20	33
16:17-18	201
17:9	139
18:6	viii, 53
20:9	67, 89
23:16-17	20
31:33	34, 62
34:22	51
51:11	94
51:20	93
51:27	94

Lamentations
3:16	169, 172

Ezekiel
1:18	237
1:28	187

Index of Scripture

3:14	90
3:26-27	90
16:6	26
16:42	128
18	136
18:4	33
20:22	94
22:21	134
25:6-7	93
28:19	208
28	60
29:18-20	94
30:24-26	93
32:15	51
34:4	213
36:24	34
36:26	130
39:17-20	189
39:23-24	201
40-48	192
43:8	208

Daniel
3:25-28	62
5:5-6	221

Hosea
8:12	82
11:1	93

Obadiah
1:7	93
1:16	148

Jonah
1:17	190
2	234

4	82, 136

Micah
7:16	81

Nahum
1:3-5	191-192

Habakkuk
2:4	85
2:14	154

Haggai
1:9	134

Zechariah
4:6	192
4:14	82
12:10	62
14:16	192

The New Testament

Matthew
2:13 21
3:11 157-158
4:7 120
4:8-9 220
4:19 97
5:1-12 219
5:3 210
5:6 166,183,193
5:10-12 200
5:13 .... 52, 54, 212
5:13-16 159
5:20 62
5:44 219
5:45 51
5:45b 33
5:48 ..... vii, 56-57, 65, 67, 110
6:1-2 22
6:9-10 70
6:10 65
6:13 210
6:13b 162
6:15 205
6:20 35
6:24 .... 48, 220
6:25-34 66
7:6a 190
7:13 166
7:14 167
7:17-19 176
7:21 64
7:24 198
8:10 97
8:26 .... 188, 221
9:37-38 159
9:38 162
10:1 151
10:20 .... 67, 224
10:27 113
10:28 124,138
10:29 190
10:37 28
11:2 162-163
11:5 152
11:28-30 180
11:29 129
11:30 34
12:31 201
12:36 34
14:28 99
15:8-9 132
15:14 29
16:15 237
16:15-16 216
16:15-23 99
16:17 .... 216, 219
16:18 .... 153, 204
16:24 .... 63, 204
17:20 185
18:34 46
19:24 220
19:26 .... 69, 139
20:21-23 205
20:25-26 53
20:28 130
22:11 130
22:27 79
22:37-38 77
23:15a 119
23:37 .... 33, 225
24:3 192
25:21 31

Index of Scripture

25:46	122
26:28	199-200, 204
26:31	97
26:33-35	205
26:39	63
27:3	157
27:5	60
27:53	192
28:18	113
28:18-20	115

Mark

4:19	220
4:26-27	147
4:39	28
7:6-7	79
7:13	126
9:18-29	75
9:29	74
9:44	125
10:17-27	42-43
10:27	x, 27
10:34	206
10:37	107
11:24	76
12:34	222
12:41-44	119
13:32	193
14:8	98
14:29	111
16:15	115
16:17-18	115

Luke

1:51	153
4:4	196-197
6:22-23	151
8:8	116
8:21	103
8:43-48	74-75
9:22-24	200
9:35	142
10:2	46, 54
10:18	91
10:38-42	24, 98
10:41-42	98
11:1-2	210
11:3	131
11:4	207
12:4	196
12:11	67
12:16-21	136
12:32	47, 212
13:1-5	x
13:2-3	51-52
13:3	35, 186, 209
13:16	222
13:18	191
13:31-32	190
14:26	164
15:11-32	202
15:17	234
16:19-31	123
16:23-25	33
17:5	73
17:10	56-57, 119, 155, 162
18:1-8	28
18:19	116
19:1-10	44-45
19:10	26
21:19	136
22:19	145
22:52	209
23:28-31	25

23:33 107	10:1-3 x
23:39-43 106-107	10:4 66
23:43 124	10:4-5 49
24:39 138	10:5 212
	10:10 .... 60, 220
John	10:14 54
1:13 .... 19, 22, 27, 39-40, 117, 197	10:15 137
	10:27 24
1:14 70	10:28-29 .... 46, 113-114
1:40-42 136	11:43 viii
3:3 .... xii, 27, 37	12:25 .... 133, 137-138
3:5 .... 133, 136	13:1-17 145-146
3:8 .... 28, 37, 54, 162, 185	13:15 63
3:16 .... 33, 42, 46, 122	13:34 78
3:17, 19 26	14:2 193
3:19-20 22	14:12 49
4:4 29	14:15 .... 76, 79
4:14 19	14:27 222
4:25 95	15:1-14 55
4:34 63	15:5 56-57
6:38 .... 24, 63	15:10 77
6:39 69	15:13 76
6:44 .... 26, 116, 136	15:16 .... 146, 167
6:63 xii	15:26 136
6:64 130	16:4b 199
6:65 116	16:23 146
6:67-70 20	17:2a 96
6:70 116	17:2 20
7:31 222	17:4 63
8:31 133	17:9-12 46
8:31-32 .... vii, 66	17:23 63
8:36 23	19:1 206
8:44a 23	19:11 .... 63, 151
8:44 .... 32, 220	20:29 219
8:56 84	21:3 120
9:1-11 119	21:6 190
10 vii	21:15 .... 28, 64

Reference	Page
21:16	120
21:18	206
21:18-19	100
21:19	206, 211

Acts

Reference	Page
1:2	215
1:4	215
1:6	108
1:7	x
1:8	56-57, 70
2:4	197, 224
2:17	178
2:20	128
2:27-31	204
2:30	22
2:37	46
2:37-38	158
2:41	212
2:47	212
3:15	87
3:16	75
3:26	38, 45
4:19	29
4:20	ix
5:1-10	203
5:3-5	205
6:2	214
6:10-11	151
6:15	206
7:55-60	206
8:20	217
8:26-39	130
8:29	61
9	36
9:1	106
9:1-6	225
9:5	116
9:10-16	61
9:13	39
9:16	207, 209
9:24-25	120
10:34	39
11:21	156
12:22-23	81
12:23	125
13:10	22
13:22	92
14:9	130
14:10	61
15:10	225
15:39	133
16:6	21
16:14	x, 114
16:30	158
17:26	160
17:27	74
19:6	215
19:9	120
20:7	152
24:15	74
26:9	67
26:14	79
26:28-29	130

Romans

Reference	Page
1:1	36
1:5	64
1:10	29
1:17	85
1:21-32	ix
1:24	176
1:24-28	32
2:1	138

2:5	146,199, 202
2:5-6	34
2:5-9	32-33
2:14	109
2:26-27	151
3:9	138
3:10	39
3:10-18	137, 139, 223
3:11	27
3:23	24, 39, 45,199
4:1-2	84
4:2	191
4:3a	137
4:9	84
4:11	84
4:11-16	225
4:19	29
4:20	x, 84,191
5:1-2	202
5:15-16	202
5:16	207
6	66
6:6	64,133
6:16	30
7	24,106
7:20	199
7:22	66
7:22-24	19
8:1	27
8:2	25, 57
8:4	77
8:5-9	224
8:5-14	66
8:6	xii, 68, 211
8:6-8	105
8:7	25, 76-77
8:9	133
8:14	24, 35
8:18	182
8:19-22	202
8:26	210
9:6	32
9:6-8	31
9:11	34, 39,147
9:19-20	42
9:20	x
9:21	viii, x, 49, 53-54, 56, 66, 78,164,169
9:28	121,164
10:1	163
10:3-4	56
10:6-10	40-41
10:9	207
10:12-13	197
10:13	27, 39,101,115, 125,156
10:14	60,116
10:14-15	41
10:15	162,185
10:17	73, 97,196
10:20	41-42,44
11:5-6	83
11:14	97
11:26-27	62
11:33	39,42
11:34	234
12:1	130,149
12:2	xiii, 56-57,63-66,70,73,105
12:3	215
13:1-2	205
13:4	97
15:18	67
16:6	xvii

Index of Scripture

16:26-27 64

1 Corinthians
1:12a 105
1:18-21 159
1:21 136
1:26-29 39
2:9-10 226
2:12 71
2:14 189
3:5 162
3:5-7 117
3:6 105
3:7 212
3:13-15 139
4:5 127
5:1-5 .... 203, 205
5:11 205
7:17 29
7:21 223
7:25 237
8:1 xiii
10:11 95
11:28-30 205
11:31 208
12:11 .... 185, 224
12:12-27 56
13:2b 185
13:3 206
13:4-8 77
13:5a 76
13:5,7 22
13:12 .... x, 128, 196
13:13 72
14:32 89
15:9 106
15:10 .... 48, 106
15:42 137
15:42-54 146
15:44a 136-137
15:44 .... 71, 133, 138, 236
15:46-49 70
15:50 137
15:50-51 137
15:51 139
15:52 xii
15:52-53 124
15:54 235
15:56 .... 137, 199
15:58 30

2 Corinthians
1:19 138
1:24 145
2:14 160
3:5-6 155-156
4:4 220
4:7 99
4:13 70
5:1 223
5:7 70
5:10 23
5:12 148
5:17 .... 27, 56-57, 64, 84, 109, 133, 226
7:1 67
9:8 110
10:4-5 135
10:5 67-68
10:12 .... 56-57, 215
11 159
11:1 46
12:1-5 137
12:7 .... 106, 224

249

12:9	99
12:10	99
13:3	20
13:5	110

Galatians

1:10	142
2:11-12	133
2:11-14	105
3:1-5	105
3:8	226
3:14	217
3:23	72
4:4	139
4:28	84
5:16-18	57
5:17	65
5:19-21	151
5:21	173
5:22	222
5:26	118
6:17	206-207

Ephesians

1	62
1:2-3	222
1:3	223, 226
1:3-5	46
1:4	27
1:5	108
1:6	130
1:13	68, 138
1:17-18	178
2:1	66, 71
2:2	23, 29, 71, 182
2:2-3	87
2:5	26, 71, 164
2:6	26
2:8	27, 72
2:8-9	27
2:10	90
2:12	32
2:15	84
3:8	105
3:20	101-102
4:9	204
4:11	145
4:12	165
4:22	64, 133, 150
4:24	84
4:27	220
5:1-2	78
5:17	80, 216
5:18	215
5:19	216
5:23	56
6:12	xi, 29
6:13	70
6:16	177

Philippians

2:2	140
2:5	63
2:5-6	68
2:7	63
2:8	63, 68
2:9	209
2:12	111
2:12-13	101
3:10	206, 209
3:10-15	211
3:13	199
3:21	xi
4:6-7	222

Index of Scripture

4:8 166
4:11 163
4:18-19 220

Colossians
1:9b-11 102
2:8 126
2:10 119
2:14 .... 137, 199
2:16 .... 153, 213
3:9 150
3:9-10 84

1 Thessalonians
2:18 22
4:12 109
4:17 .... 71, 210
5:2 108
5:23-24 222

2 Thessalonians
1:8-9 121
3:3 73

1 Timothy
1:14 77
1:15 .... 40, 105, 206-207
2:1-2 222
2:4 .... 39, 197-198
2:8 75
3:1-10 145
4:2 21
4:12-16 148
5:8 180
5:16 118
5:18 xvii
5:20 149

5:25 149
6:10 220
6:15-16 123-124
6:16 .... 135, 235

2 Timothy
1:5 221
2:15 108
3:3 60
3:5 151
3:12 206
3:15-17 105
3:16 105
3:16-17 63
3:17 67
4:10 114

Titus
2:11-14 182
3:5 xii

Hebrews
1:3 73
2:4 97
4:2 45
4:12 .... 45, 64, 138
4:13 .... 23, 34-35, 87, 221
5:8-9 204
5:12-14 35
6:1 115
6:4 204
6:4-6 111-114
6:19 115
8:7 .... 88, 96
8:8 34
9 204
9:12 138

9:14	22, 199, 221
9:22	204
9:27	20
9:28	199-200
10:2	221
10:14	206
10:14-16	84
10:14-17	56
10:22	221
10:24-25	213
10:26	200-201, 207
10:26-31	202, 204
10:30	207
10:39	133
11	73, 82, 109
11:1	72, 84, 159
11:1-3	73
11:6	73-74, 95
11:17-19	84
11:19	64
11:40	73
12:2	vii, 31, 63, 87, 100, 207
12:2-10	206
12:8	203
12:29	125
13:4	207
13:8	69
13:17	145

James

1:13-14	220
1:17	225
1:27	165
2:5	39, 86
2:17	101
2:20	158, 197
2:26	52, 73
3:8	186, 210
3:9	219
3:13-4:13	221
4:15	24
5:11	76
5:17	57
5:16	154
5:19-20	134

1 Peter

1:5	73, 211
1:6-7	xi
1:7	76
1:8	22
2:5	130
2:9	215
2:10	66
2:20a	203
4:1	208
4:1-2	204
4:15	133
4:17a	204
4:17	202
5:8	22

2 Peter

1:2	197
1:4	76
2:8	176
2:9	x
3:4	184, 197
3:5	187
3:5-7	184
3:6	197
3:9	39-40, 64, 197, 225
3:10a	108
3:10-13	193

3:18 212

1 John
1:8-10 207
2:2 201
2:5 63
2:12 108
2:20 140
3:2 .... vii, xi, 71-72,122
3:9 65,133
3:12 21
4:1 29,152
4:8 76
4:18 77,222
5:16 203
5:17 205

3 John
1:2 220

Jude
1:7 60
1:20 210

Revelation
1:3 219
2:5 157
3:16 194
3:17 31,101
4:3 .... 187, 237
4:10 61
6:10 137
10:1 237
10:6 128
10:6b 192
11:15 72
12:9 186
12:11 68
14:9-12 152
16:15a 108
19:6b-7 226-227
20:4 137
20:7-9 192
20:8 94
20:10 122,128,146
20:12 20,23
20:15 122
21 193
21:3 94,138
21:4,8 137
21:21 24
21:24-26 94
22:14 122

253

Index

Activation 59,61-62,73,233
Allman Brothers Band 67
Annihilation .... xiii, 121,123,125, 139,153
Arminianism 143-144
Backsliding 93,203
Bait car 19-20
Baptist 118,135,143,146,148, 152,157-158,162,167,179-180
Beautification .... xiii, 59,62-64, 73,233
Berlin, Irving 225
Boltz, Ray 206
Bonhoeffer, Dietrich 67,234
Calvinism 143-144,147,150, 153,238
Calvin, John 38,126,143,151, 233,236
Catholic 126,129,142-146, 152-153,208
Christian Science xi,231
Church of God 148
Communion 144-145,205,237
Consummation 59,68,73
Contentment 159,162-163
DNA 75,101,221
Dordt in the Netherlands 143
Entropy 192-193
Eternal retribution 121-122,125, 127,129
Evolution 78,146-147,151, 184,236
Fatalist 181
Fictitious 160,163
Fictional .... vii, 127,176

Force .... x, 26,40,49,53,62,64, 90,140,153,192,212,233-234
Gnosticism xiii
Grand Canyon 184
Grand Funk 173
Great Commission 115-120
Hagee, John 40
Heresy .... viii, 25
Homosexuality 151
Immortality of the soul 123-124, 135,147,190, 236
Jehovah Witness 129,135
Kilmer, Joyce 188
Luther, Martin 126,140,232,236
Manning, Peyton 21,232
Microevolution 185
Muslim 116
Patterson, Paige 38
Prayer 29,64,75,80,103, 120,150,156,164,170,175,179, 207, 210, 215, 221-222
Presbyterian 146,150-151,177
Rainbow sky .... xii, 147,187,237
Seventh Day Adventist 127,146, 152-153
Soul winner .... xii, 132-139
Speculate/speculation 46,59, 89-90,101,175,186,237
Stanley, Charles 166,237
Swaggart, Jimmy 235
Trinity 70
Uniformitarianism 184
Wesley, John 126,146,225
Whitefield, George 225

CPSIA information can be obtained at www.ICGtesting.com
Printed in the USA
LVOW05s0442101213

364577LV00006B/19/P